EMPLOYEE

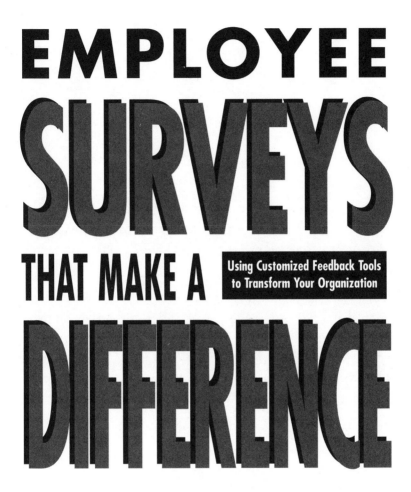

SURVEYS

THAT MAKE A

Using Customized Feedback Tools to Transform Your Organization

DIFFERENCE

JOE FOLKMAN, PH.D.

The publisher offers discounts on this book when ordered in bulk quantities. To place your order, or to get more information about Novations, Joe Folkman, or the survey instruments described in this book, please contact Novations Group, Inc., at:

Novations Group, Inc.
5314 North 250 West, Suite 320
Provo, UT 84604
phone: (801) 375-7525
fax: (801) 375-7595
www.novations.com

Editorial/Design/Production:

Executive Excellence Publishing
1344 East 1120 South
Provo, UT 84604
phone: (801) 375-4060
fax: (801) 377-5960
www.eep.com

ISBN: 1-890009-43-1

ENDORSEMENTS

"Joe Folkman has found a way to make a technical subject interesting and readable. He writes in a way that managers will find clear and practical. Anyone who is engaged in administering employee surveys would benefit from reading this book."

—Paul McKinnon, Vice President, Human Resources
Dell Computer Corporation

"If you're beginning an employee survey, this book will provide a hundred valuable tips. If you are already conducting surveys, you will enjoy using this resource to validate, benchmark, and gain new insights from your surveys."

—Ron Burbridge, Vice President of Human Resource Effectiveness,
Canadian Imperial Bank of Commerce

"At last, someone has provided a prescription for creating surveys that make a difference. Folkman shows us through straightforward language, with business examples and engaging analogies, how business leaders can use surveys to transform their organizations."

—Jim LaRocco, Vice President of Human Resource
Development, The GAP, Inc.

"Joe Folkman's book shows us what we must consider, what steps we must take, and what roles must be played in order to make a true difference with employee surveys. His insights keep us grounded on what really works."

—Bob Hargadon, Vice President of Executive
Development, Boston Scientific

"Folkman does a wonderful job of describing the practice *and* science, and the art *and* science, of managing increased effectiveness through surveys. He deftly illustrates that a stream of events in concert is what makes the difference."

—Todd A. VanNest, Group Vice President of
Organizational Effectiveness,
Norwest Mortgage, Inc.

"Employee Surveys that Make a Difference is a 'must read' for anyone about to embark on an organizational survey process. Joe provides practical advice on the steps necessary to successfully implement a survey. Where many processes fail, this book provides valuable insights on how to utilize surveys as organizational tools to obtain business results."

—David Lundgren, Senior Vice President, Human Resources;
Priscilla A. Muniz, Vice President, Executive Development;
Linda C. Ryan, Development Consultant,
Fireman's Fund Insurance Company

"Using the principles in this book, we created a survey that focused on the key drivers of our business success. That survey process was an important element in our winning the Malcolm Baldrige National Quality Award in 1998."

—Mary Settle, Staff Director of HRM Planning, Selection, and
Organization Development—Airlift and Tanker Programs, Boeing

"The employee survey process is a powerful organizational tool to shape and create competitive advantage through people. Joe's book is a 'practitioner's classroom,' full of insight and experience that will sharpen and refine your ability to use employee surveys to effectively produce organization change."

—Mark Walus, Manager, Organizational Metrics,
Cisco Systems Inc.

ACKNOWLEDGMENTS

The insights in this book are built on a foundation of knowledge and experience that came from my collaborations with many people and organizations. Although it would be impossible to mention everyone who contributed ideas or helped to shape the contents, I wish to acknowledge a few people who played significant roles.

From my graduate studies, I thank Kay Smith, Darhl Pederson, and David Stimpson, and graduate school colleagues Terry Illes, David Hatch, Don Herren, and Rich Millard.

I feel a special debt of gratitude for two long-time partners and professors, who took me on as a partner and who began the business of assessing employee perceptions: Gene Dalton and Bill Dyer. Gene and Bill both passed away in 1997, but their influence and ideas continue.

I also thank my associates who have worked with me in analyzing and processing survey results: Linda Christensen, Kerri Price, Fang Zhong, Nate Bowler, Angela Bass, Paul Fisher, and Coray Christensen.

Several of the chapters in this book draw on the work that Novations has done in the field of strategy. I gratefully acknowledge the principal architects of that work: Norm Smallwood, Jon Younger, and Randy Stott. (Many of their ideas and approaches are incorporated into Chapters 1, 2, 5, and 8. Norm also worked collaboratively with me on Chapter 2. And the high-commitment model presented in Chapter 5 came out of a research project directed by Randy. Thank you all.)

Others, including Ryan Miller, Linda Christensen, and Brandon Folkman, helped with research and editing. To them, and to my editors and publishers at Executive

Excellence Publishing, Trent Price and Ken Shelton, who encouraged and supported my ideas—thank you.

I would also like to remember and acknowledge my clients, without whom none of this would have been possible. Too numerous to mention here are the many individuals at 3M, AGT, Amoco, AT&T, Boeing, CIBC, Cisco Systems, Conoco, Eaton, Ericsson Communications, Exxon, Fireman's Fund Insurance Company, Frito-Lay, General Mills, Harley Davidson, Hercules, Hewlett-Packard, IBM, KFC, Lockheed, Lyondell-Citgo, McGraw-Hill, Merck, H. Muehlstein, Mobil, Norwest Mortgage, Novell, Nortel, PepsiCo Restaurants International, Pepsi-Cola, Pizza Hut, Progressive Insurance, Rockwell, Weyerhaueser, and a host of smaller companies.

Finally, I appreciate the support and assistance of my wife and children. Several of these chapters were written while on family vacations. Others were written in the evening or late at night while they took care of things I should have been doing. Thank you very much.

CONTENTS

FOREWORD

By Jack Zenger

Ever since I was eight years old, I have been interested in magic as a performing art. As a teenager I would frequent magic shops, and later, when I began traveling on business, I would stop in to see magic stores around the world. I have always been fascinated with the consistent behavior I observe in the customers at these stores, wherever I was: A customer would come in, stand around a few moments while glancing halfheartedly at the shelves, and then ask the clerk, "So, what new tricks do you have?" In response, the clerk would show the latest card or coin trick.

I soon realized that these customers ask the wrong question. Rather than asking, "What's new?" they should ask, "What's good?" After all, many new tricks are not particularly good. The classic effects of magic survive because they have a good plot, are visually appealing, and their methods stand the test of time. That's why they are the backbone of most professional magicians' repertoires.

Employee surveys are not new, either. They have been around, in some form or another, for a long time. And, because of that, many people do not get excited about them. But this is a great mistake because employee surveys—especially when conducted the way Joe Folkman recommends—are really good.

I know of only a few things that truly have a long-term impact on companies and the people who work in them.

For example, well-designed training interventions often have power to change behavior. Personalized coaching and mentoring can also make a difference. Thoughtfully designed reward systems can effectively mold behavior in organizations. Changing how a company is structured can sometimes help, too. But one of the most powerful, yet economical, ways to make dramatic changes in both organizations and individuals is through surveys and the activities that follow them.

To draw a parallel analogy, all books on how to lose weight basically say the same things: Consume less (of something); exercise more. Why? Those are the only two things that are found to work well in the long run. The books that promise to reveal a dramatic new way to shed pounds by consuming some drug, or a bizarre combination of foods, may all have their 15 minutes of glory and then disappear. But the authors who understand the long-term effectiveness of the various approaches will generally say the same things.

Joe Folkman's book is extraordinary, because it not only gives the best common sense advice that will endure the test of time, it goes beyond the usual guidelines for designing and administering surveys. It combines both the art and science behind employee surveys and then takes the whole thing to an entirely new level. This book shows how employee surveys can predict business outcomes and accelerate (and add focus to) the entire change process. The value of the tools in this book, which will enable executives and consultants to predict future business outcomes, falls into the same category as tools that would enable physicians to predict if and when a patient will have a heart attack.

Years ago, I developed a passion for employee surveys and feedback when I was vice president of human resources for a pharmaceutical company. The company had an executive (I'll call him "Ed") whose division was not performing well. Part of this poor performance was a result of Ed's personal behavior, as well as the culture that had been established in that part of the company. The division was slow-moving, insulated from the other departments, and lacked direction. The people in the division waited to be told what to do. Creativity was stifled. The company tried various training methods, including team-building and large group interventions. Ed was sent to a university-sponsored executive program and to multi-week "T-Groups." Nothing changed.

Then the company conducted an employee survey and the results were reported to all executives. The results of each division were compared to the organization as a whole. The feedback included information from the survey about management and leadership behavior. Immediately we began to see profound changes in Ed and, later, in his group. He began to involve people in decisions. He listened and delegated more, and gave people more encouragement rather than more orders.

None of our previous efforts had made a dent in Ed or his group, and yet this relatively simple (and certainly less expensive) procedure resulted in enormous changes in him and his division. Why? Objective information that contradicts our self-image is incredibly powerful. I believe that whenever we are confronted with such information we are faced with a simple choice. We must either accept the fact that we are different than we thought, or we must change our behavior. In Ed's case, he either had to accept the fact that he really was an autocratic, smothering executive or change his behavior and stop acting like one. He had to do one or the other. The data was compelling, and it was now out in the open. Like Ed, for most of us it is easier to change our behavior in a few areas than to change how we perceive ourselves, or at least how we prefer to perceive ourselves. In addition, Ed was a highly competitive person. When he saw that his scores were considerably lower than the rest of the organization, he could not bear to live with the stigma. So he worked hard to fix it.

This book tells you everything you need to know to make the employee survey process work to produce solid results. It is a complete handbook; it is not a list of generic questions for you to use in creating a survey. What you get is far more valuable. You get guidance on the right kind of survey to administer, how to organize your efforts and your team to make it happen, how to conduct the survey and analyze the results you obtain, and how to lead the entire change process that cascades out of the process. Folkman distills his 20 years of experience into one extremely helpful volume.

This book tells you how to add the powerful "magic" of employee surveys to your repertoire. I encourage you to use them, and to follow the guidelines that Folkman suggests, because surveys really can make a difference in your organization. And that is what most of us keep getting up in the morning to accomplish.

INTRODUCTION

A rather negative hotel manager wrote: "The problem I have with surveys is that once we gather all the data and analyze the results, people expect me to make all the changes. I can't change everything. I didn't create the problems, so why do people expect me to solve them?"

To managers who have been involved in employee surveys, this probably sounds familiar. Although employee feedback can pinpoint where changes in an organization are needed, and while such feedback can help managers understand employee opinions, most survey processes take a lot of time, offer widely varied results, and often lack specific details about what to do and how best to use the feedback.

Nevertheless, a well-constructed survey provides a vehicle for employees to share their perspectives and opinions. But not all organizations and their employees have positive experiences with surveys. In fact, most people in organizations tend to express negative opinions of surveys, rather than positive ones. Here are a few examples:

• A union employee at an equipment manufacturing plant said, "Why should we take time to complete these surveys? They make no difference. Managers ignore the results and the boss just files them on the shelf. I've never seen anything happen from these surveys."

• A supervisor at a food products plant said, "I have no idea how to interpret or use this stuff. These surveys have nothing to do with the day-to-day problems I face."

• A bank clerk said, "I think they use the surveys to find the employees who are negative and then fire them. But these days it's not called firing—it's 'downsizing.' The surveys don't help the employees. Managers just use them to keep employees in line."

• A software engineer said, "I'm too busy doing real work to spend time completing this survey. It might be useful, but I just don't see how it will help."

• A manager in a fast-food restaurant said, "I get some survey to complete at least once or twice a month. It takes time away from my job. Why do we need so many surveys?"

Raising Expectations

Employee surveys generate expectations. Each time employees answer a question or provide suggestions for change, they develop an expectation that some change will occur as a result. When organizations conduct surveys and then do not respond to the results, many employees feel frustrated, feeling that management has taken advantage of them.[1]

Often, people think of employee surveys as a harmless way to gather opinions without raising any expectations. If you think this is true, and if you are married, try the following experiment: Explain to your spouse that you are conducting some social research and that as part of the research you would like to ask a question. The question is: "How would you feel if I had an extramarital affair? (a) Angry, (b) Neutral, or (c) Not Angry." Your spouse may answer the question, but will also immediately question your motives. The question will not likely result in a neutral response. In the same light, asking employees if they are happy with their pay, benefits, career opportunities, workload, or life balance will only create expectations of change or cause them to question your motives.

As a result of greater employee expectations, managers and executives often feel overwhelmed. It is not possible to make all the changes recommended by employees in a survey, and many of the issues, from management's perspective, seem to be related to making employees happier rather than improving productivity or efficiency. Therefore, many managers become frustrated with the results of surveys because they feel that employee feedback does not pertain to the work at hand.

For both employees and executives, conducting employee surveys can generate many other unanswered questions, such as:

- Can organizations ever satisfy the expectations generated by employee surveys?
- Can companies generate enthusiasm among all employees participating in surveys?
- When is the right time to conduct a survey?
- What questions should be asked?
- Since surveys also provide massive amounts of data, can organizations ever use surveys to determine the issues that would make the greatest impact on the company?
- How should surveys be interpreted? What issues are important? What can be ignored?
- How does the survey data from one organization compare to norms or trends for similar companies?
- What is the best way to share the results of a survey with employees?
- Can organizations change and improve as a result of survey feedback?
- What competitive advantages can surveys offer the companies that use them?

Adding Value with Surveys

This book will attempt to answer each of these questions. But, to begin with, surveys can add significant value to companies in several ways:

1. Surveys provide consistent feedback from all employees on a given set of issues. Recently, I attended a performance of my daughter's sixth-grade chorus. As the program began, all the students stood up and sang. I looked at my daughter in admiration. At that moment I noticed that she was about one foot taller than the other students in the class. I had never noticed this before. It was only when I saw the direct comparison that the difference became evident.

Leaders of organizations have the same difficulty in noticing differences between their company and others. Being around their own employees every day, they become familiar with them and fail to sense their unique differences, attitudes, and opinions. And, once an organization grows beyond a few employees, it becomes even more difficult for leaders to keep an accurate pulse of their companies. Leaders tend to lose touch over time as to where their employees stand on critical issues. But well-designed employee surveys can do much to solve this problem.

2. Surveys present the opinions of the entire organization at a specific point in time. Although there are many ways to uncover employee opinions (interviews, informal group discussions, focus groups), none seem to be as efficient as employee surveys. Interviews, for example, are an excellent way to gather firsthand information from employees and to discuss their concerns and recommendations. But the interview process is extraordinarily time consuming. It is also difficult to understand trends and measure differences between groups. And interviews can go in so many different directions that, after a long series of interviews, compiling an accurate summary of the results may be very difficult and time consuming. Twenty interviews may yield 100 pages or more of comments, and without careful and consistent wording of interview questions, making comparisons between even two interviews can be difficult.

In contrast, employee surveys present the same issues to all employees. The ability to easily chart, interpret, and compare data is one of the great advantages of surveys. Ratings of particular issues and comparisons between groups are relatively easy. And open-ended questions can be inserted in surveys to allow for some of the comments and suggestions available in interviews, with lower costs and greater accuracy.

3. Surveys clearly reveal the organization's strengths and opportunities for improvement. Because of the opportunities for analysis afforded by well-constructed surveys, careful interpretation of a survey at the management level can reveal strategic, systemic, or structural changes necessary to make the organization more productive. The same survey used at the work group level can provide supervisors with insights into how they can communicate better, make more informed decisions, accurately assess employee performance, and involve employees in planning. And, by using the survey both at management and work group levels, companies can significantly improve their ability to foster meaningful changes.

Survey data may be used objectively with data from a national pool, providing comparisons with other demographic groups, locations, and benchmarks. Such analysis can help identify the precise location and intensity of problems in the organization. Aggregate data, gathered over time, can add precise measures of progress toward goals or targets.

Many managers have developed both formal and informal ways of keeping in touch with their employees. But, even in ideal situations, most managers are unaware of how employee concerns become filtered—that is, if those concerns are expressed at all. Yet such concerns often impact employee performance, morale, and customer and supplier interactions.

When surveys are structured to ensure that managers become aware of employee concerns, they can be powerful tools. The act of conducting a survey indicates that management values the employees and their ideas. Surveys also permit managers to identify barriers to productivity and a more rewarding work environment. Once such barriers are identified, action plans may be developed to address them in a positive and cooperative manner.

Keys to Employee Surveys That Make a Difference

This book introduces you to key concepts that will help you create, conduct, and respond to employee surveys in a way that will make a positive difference for your company. Too many of the survey projects conducted today are less than adequate. Some actually do more harm than good. Conducting a survey properly can create significant value for an organization, and a properly conducted survey includes the following:

Measure the right things. Design your survey to measure the key issues that most employees and managers agree upon which, if improved, would clearly improve the organization. When neither managers or employees can see the links between the issues being measured in the survey and the critical issues that drive the organization forward, the value of the survey is substantially diminished. Rather than suggest obscure links to pacify this problem (such as "happy employees are more productive"), I recommend that companies establish a direct link between the survey and the critical measures of company performance.

Not every issue that is necessary for an organization's success can be measured by employee surveys, but many may be effectively evaluated and then improved.

Strive to predict business outcomes. Employee survey data becomes compelling when survey measurements can predict organizational performance. For example, it's exciting to discover that the groups which scored highest on a survey also generated more profit, had lower turnover, produced greater customer satisfaction, increased productivity, and so on. Surveys that measure the right things can predict these and other desired outcomes. To find significant correlations is more difficult for some organizations than it is for others, and finding the right correlations often requires substantial experimentation to discover the right measures and survey items.

Figure I.1 shows a profitability measure that directly correlates with the results of an employee survey. Profitability is indicated in the left margin, with the lowest scores showing the highest profit.

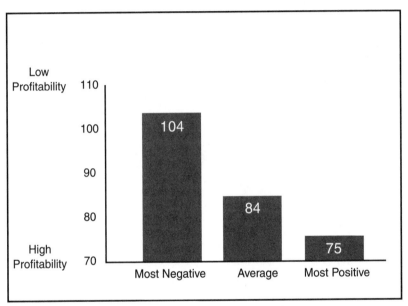

Figure I.1: Profit Index Scale (lower scores show higher profit).

Groups were classed into Negative, Average, or Positive classifications. The groups that scored most negatively on the survey also had the worst profits (indicated by the high index), while those that scored most positively on the survey generated the most profits (indicated by the low score on the index). The survey included approximately 60 items and measured 9 dimensions in which there was strong agreement that the issues being measured determined both long- and short-term profitability.

Make the survey a force for change. Employee surveys that make a difference are those that bring about change and organizational improvement. Without change efforts and the resulting improvements, surveys are merely a paper-passing exercise. For example, although it may be interesting to know that the overall satisfaction of employees went down 10 percent in the last six months, the measure has no value unless something is done about the data. Surveys can be rewarding when action (conducting a survey) is followed by a reaction (change).

Modify surveys over time. Surveys that make a difference must evolve over time. They must mirror the changes and demands placed on the organization. Once a good survey is established and the organization becomes comfortable with its contents, many companies build databases of results over time. Comparisons and improvements become easier to show. But changes occur over time in what the organization does, what competitors are doing, or what customers expect. And these changes can be dramatic. Allowing a survey to become stale leads to the question, "Why are we doing a survey?"

Start with small successes. Sometimes, responding to and creating changes based on the results of an employee survey can seem overwhelming. Actually, most employee populations, because of past experience (whether in your organization or another), do not expect to see much happen. They have been told about change efforts in the past— new programs, initiatives, or projects that never seemed to deliver. Many employees have become cynical in their outlook about organizational change. For this reason, it is critical that the organization change something—even if it is a small change. By restoring employee confidence through small changes, the company can begin to build the organizational faith to make a substantial change.

Focus energy on creating optimal leverage. When you can move beyond small changes, a key to using employee surveys effectively is to focus the company's energy on the most influential survey results, thereby leading to the greatest organizational leverage. Rather than merely focusing on the most negative survey results, effective survey committees will identify survey results that will ultimately have the greatest impact on organizational performance.

Organizations do not have an unlimited supply of energy. Wasting effort on the wrong issues is not only an ineffective use of resources, but it also represents a significant opportunity cost of not changing the critical variables that would have created a competitive advantage.

Doing it "right" takes commitment. To be effective, employee surveys will always require time, effort, commitment, and resources. The best designed survey with little commitment will be a failure.

After reviewing a proposal to conduct a survey "the right way," one manager commented, "This looks like a lot of work!"

I responded, "You're absolutely right. It's going to take a lot of work."

He replied, "I'm just not that committed to doing this." And he canceled the survey. It was a good decision. The survey would never have worked unless he could provide the right funding, the right resources, and the employee time to make it work.

Identify the root causes of issues. Take special effort to design your survey to uncover the root causes of the issues you face. Most surveys measure issues at the "leaves" (symptoms) rather than at the "roots" (causes). For example, many managers typically find that employees perceive their companies as "poor in communication." But problems in communication are rarely solved by talking more— more meetings, newsletters, memos, or other messages. The root-cause of communication problems may be that people don't trust the messages sent, or that there is inconsistency between messages and actions—saying one thing but doing another. To change these issues, the root-cause must first be uncovered, and then change efforts must address that root-cause.

Analysis can lead to wisdom. Great wisdom may be found in survey data. Too often, this wisdom remains hidden. The only way to uncover the hidden wisdom is through careful analysis. Problems initially identified by the survey become much clearer, and root causes are easier to identify through analysis. The most common problem with analysis is that it is often presented as a series of complicated statistics, adding neither insight nor understanding. Good analysis not only looks at the data carefully and systematically, but it leads to a simple explanation for the underlying issues.

Make the survey a part of the business. Ultimately, for employee surveys to make a difference they must become a standard part of how a company does business, rather than a deviation from regular work. By measuring the right issues, managers and employees can make the connections between survey results and how to improve performance. This does not happen automatically when surveys are conducted. Managers and employees at all levels need to learn how to build the survey results into their businesses. Action plans based on survey results then become part of the goals and plans of the organization. Measurement, review, and analysis of results become a regular activity.

Make it work. The primary reason surveys are successful is that managers and employees make them work. I was recently asked, "What changes can we expect when we conduct an employee survey?" I was tempted to say, "Nothing." Conducting a survey doesn't create change; instead, surveys measure the issues that ought to change. In employee surveys that make a difference, both employees and managers are enthusiastic about making the project work. Conversely, when enough managers and employees feel the process is a waste of time, it will be virtually impossible to make it work.

Learning occurs every year. Organizations that use surveys learn from the process over time. Learning occurs not only in analysis, but also in responding to survey items. When asked to evaluate the organization's effectiveness on critical issues, they sometimes respond with what they think others want to hear rather than what they should hear. But, after a few years of taking surveys, new and more candid responses may arise.

One organization that was considered very innovative found its employee survey scores on innovation actually went down over time. As the managers in the company tried to understand why, they found that employees had initially given the company the benefit of the doubt (or maybe the employees had learned more about what it means to "think outside the box"). In the following years, the employees became more critical raters because they really cared about what they were rating. They became the company's toughest critics. The results led to profound improvements.

Establish limited expectations up front. Make it known that the survey will measure many issues but change only a few. Too often, employees expect that everything measured will be changed. The reality is that if the organization were to take on too many issues to change, effective change would not occur. Employees need to know up front that the survey will focus on a few critical issues.

Make it simple. Surveys that make a difference are simple, easy to understand, and quick to review. They do not interrupt the flow of business, but become a natural part of how business is done in the company. Some survey efforts seem to collapse under their own weight. The survey is long and measures too many issues. The reports are complex, the analysis is overwhelming, and feedback is time consuming. By the time people can respond to the results, they are either too tired or too confused to do anything. Some companies even stop everything to conduct their surveys. Rather than giving the survey emphasis, it creates resentment.

Share results widely. Surveys that provide feedback only to the top executive will have only one chance for generating change. But surveys that provide feedback to 100 managers, at all levels of the organization, will have 100 or more chances. Changes can be generated more effectively by involving more people at more levels. After all, the changes that people notice are those made in their own work groups.

Do not measure issues you are not willing to change. This question needs to be asked before including an item in a survey: "If this issue were responded to negatively, would you change it?" For many items, the answer is "No." Yet these same items continue to appear in surveys. Consequently, employees continue to indicate they are not satisfied, and nothing changes.

The most common example relates to satisfaction with pay or compensation. In the many years I have been conducting surveys, I have yet to see a positive response to this question at the company level. Most companies adjust employee compensation based on an annual pay survey that indicates compensation for similar jobs in other companies. Continuing to ask the survey item only frustrates employees and puts managers in a difficult position.

Success makes people happy. In the past, many efforts were made to show the impact of happy employees on productivity and efficiency. Whether the results of those efforts were true or not, many organizations have continued the quest to make their employees happy. Most of these initiatives eventually lose traction because those who have the power to make changes fail to see how employee happiness would solve the company's day-to-day problems. Surveys that only measure "happiness" tend to distract from the real work of the company, rather than serve as tools to help them do their jobs.

More recently, we've found that success is what makes employees happy. If organizations focus their efforts on the issues that lead to success, three things happen:

1. *Executives and managers are more committed to change as a result of survey issues.* They are more willing because making the changes recommended by the survey makes their jobs easier and helps them solve day-to-day problems.

2. *Employees see the resulting change as positive because it helps them solve their day-to-day problems, too.* And, although it would be nice to be paid more or find more work-life balance, employees are more frustrated by the failures and problems they experience at work when such problems go unsolved. Creating success in the workplace makes everyone's job more enjoyable.

3. *The issues measured end up being the same issues that came out of all the happiness research.* The difference is that there is now a vital connection between the survey issues and the business of the company.

After reviewing their issues carefully, one organization concluded that to succeed it would need to retain its best employees. An analysis was conducted to determine why employees were leaving the organization. The result: lack of career development. If the employees believed the company would provide a clear development path and opportunities for promotion or training, they were more likely to stay with the organization. New survey items were designed to measure these issues. Managers were eager to make changes because it became clear that doing these things well meant that the best performers would stay with the organization.

This book covers several critical concepts related to conducting effective employee surveys. The book begins with the secret to successful surveys: Chapter 1 shows how to use surveys for diagnosing strategic alignment and identifying competitive advantages. In Chapter 2, I discuss the various approaches to conducting surveys and the unique outcome each approach yields. I show how the approach you select can influence the outcome you desire. Chapter 3 moves on to timing: When and how often should you conduct employee surveys? Chapter 4 discusses the design of your employee survey and the cause-and-effect relationships and tradeoffs that impact the outcome of surveys. In Chapter 5, the key to success with employee surveys is presented: the steering committee. Steering committees are often the best means of gaining both help and support for management in carrying off strategic change and alignment in the company, and in Chapter 5 I present some guidelines for putting together a high-performance committee to design your employee survey.

While the first five chapters have to do with the setup of your employee survey, the next two chapters deal with the survey itself and what to do with the results. Chapter 6 reveals the essential steps to conducting employee surveys. And, since understanding how your results compare to norms is important in interpreting your data, I cover the interpretation of trends in survey data in Chapter 7.

The final three chapters cover critical issues for using your survey data to lead change in your company. Much of the time, the issues that present themselves in survey data are not actually the root causes of organizational problems or concerns. Thus, Chapter 8 deals with root-cause analysis, a technique to get to the core issues of your survey that are not always apparent in the results. Chapter 9 is a pragmatic approach to leading organizational change that relies on a variety of "change levers" which increase the probability of meaningful change. In the final chapter, Chapter 10, I present some new research on the fundamental skills necessary for leaders to create organizational change. One final tool in the Appendix, the "Readiness for Change" profile, helps you determine if you are ready to move ahead with your employee survey.

Notes to Introduction

1. David A. Nadler, *Feedback and Organization Development: Using Data-Based Methods*. Reading, MA: Addison-Wesley, 1977, 65.

CHAPTER ONE

Designing Surveys for Strategic Alignment and Competitive Advantage

Even in the past few years, our business environment has changed rapidly. In the old days, life was simple and easy. Today we face complex challenges: higher quality, increasing speed, lower costs, more efficient product development, shorter product lives, larger mergers and acquisitions, more important global markets and competitors, and more expensive labor. These changes are resulting in flatter corporate structures, more effective cross-functional or semi-autonomous work teams, more vendor collaborations and TQM (Total Quality Management) programs, newer and less expensive information systems, more frequent restructuring, earlier retirement, greater focus through outsourcing, and the selling off of noncore business units.

The old business environment was a great place to work: we consultants could measure esoteric, unrelated, loosely coupled things. Organizations would allow researchers to study employee happiness and find general correlations between satisfaction and corporate profitability, turnover, waste, or whatever seemed appropriate. But the new business environment has made people more serious. Today, we don't have time to experiment and look for some association between a survey measure and possible drivers of business success. Businesses need to know exactly what surveys are supposed to measure and how they can be effectively linked to performance or strategy. And they can't wait five years for the results of a survey to take effect. In five years they may be out of business. Surveys have to solve the problems businesses face *today*.

One of the problems business leaders face is strategic alignment. Employee surveys can be helpful for diagnosing misalignments in both the organization and its strategy. Realigning an organization and aligning the organization with its strategy can help to create competitive advantages.

Organizational Alignment

Imagine two bicycles sharing a front wheel and facing each other. This is what misalignment would look like if we could see it (see Figure 1.1). Consider, then, what would happen if one person sat on each bicycle and pedaled. A lot of energy would be expended, but there would be little or no movement in any direction.

Figure 1.1: Carelman's Tandem "Convergent Bicycle (Model for Fiancés)." © Copyright 1969-76-80 by Jacques Carelman and A.D.A.G.P. Paris. From Jacques Carelman, Catalog of Unfindable Objects (Paris: Balland). Used by permission of the artist.

Misalignment absorbs or misdirects energy, and that energy is lost. In the old business environment, we might have coped with this loss because of the lack of competitive pressure, but in the new environment the same loss represents our competitors' gain.

McKinsey's 7-S framework is one way to determine organizational alignment.[1] Each of the seven aspects of an organization must be aligned: strategy (philosophy), structure (how people are organized), shared values (culture), systems (compensation systems, information systems, production systems), staff (the people), style (management style, production style), and skills (the distinctive competencies of the organization). In turn, each aspect must be aligned in the competitive business environment. In this model, misalignment may occur in three ways:

1. The strategy may be aligned with the business environment while other conditions are aligned differently. An organization with a misalignment problem may have a functional structure (manufacturing, sales, finance, human resources, information systems, R&D) that changes its strategy because of competitive pressure to get new products to market more quickly. But changing strategy without considering the other areas (such as organizational structure, reward systems, company culture, or employee skills) may lead to a loss of energy. To prevent this loss, the organization first considers the barriers to bringing new products to market faster.

By using an employee survey, the organization can quickly identify the other concerns related to changing strategy: (1) a better structure may be required to allow for more efficient passoffs from one work group to another or for more collaboration between groups; (2) systems may need to be realigned to reward people for different results, namely speed; (3) different skills may need to be refined— rather than functional experts staffing each department, perhaps the experts can collaborate to design teams with cross-functional perspectives; and (4) this may lead to an entirely different style or different shared values. The survey measures perceptions about what developments will be desired and rewarded.

2. A company may have multiple strategies, causing confusion or lack of focus. While an organization may have one explicit strategy, it may have several implicit strategies. The implicit strategies are the ones that employees implement after the explicit strategy is announced.

One company described its strategy: "We want to be the low-cost leader in the industry," and continued to describe additional goals such as, "We also want to be rated highest in customer service, highest in quality, and fastest in getting new products to market." As a result, each employee had a different interpretation of the company's strategy.

Organizations can rarely align themselves around three or more different strategies. For example, if one strategy focuses on a certain kind of customer, another on low manufacturing costs, and a third on high product quality, the three strategies will make alignment very difficult. Misalignment creates conflict in the organization as employees decide what they should do on their own. The result, again, is a loss of energy. A survey may be used to measure how employees make tradeoffs between implicit and explicit strategies when all cannot be satisfied.

3. Everything may be properly aligned but out of alignment with the business environment. This is what I call the "buggy-whip" example: Everything works perfectly for creating a product no one will want a few years from now. In such cases, surveys may be used to measure the perceptions of customers from year to year.

Strategic Alignment and Organizational Focus

Strategic alignment occurs when an organization is aligned with its strategy. Strategic alignment is missing when an organization has a clear strategy but does not execute it properly. If an organization can achieve strategic alignment, it may benefit from the following:

Clarity: Management and employees share "one" vision of the future.

Focus: Companies allocate adequate resources in desired areas.

Consensus: Decisions—even those made by frontline employees independent of management—are consistent with strategy. Everybody "sings from the same songbook."

Cohesion: Key players who execute strategy avoid striking off in their own directions.

Commitment: People support the strategy even when it means fewer resources in their area.

Filter: The strategy guides daily operating decisions and reduces nonessential activities.

In addition to organizational and strategic alignment, another contributor to competitive advantage is organizational focus. Organizations that have a multiple focus can also lose energy. For example, suppose an executive gives a speech on the importance of quality one week, sends a memo to managers about controlling costs a few weeks later, and then becomes visibly upset upon finding out a team hasn't met its schedule. The employees will feel that top management wants it all, to be "excellent in everything." (Certainly there's nothing wrong with being excellent in everything, but people have to focus on one thing at a time. To raise quality, for instance, companies must use more expensive components and add quality checks, which raise costs.)

But most "excellent" companies are *not* excellent in everything. They achieve excellence in a few things, and in fact have glaring weaknesses in other areas. To gain focus, companies must first define the relationship they have with their customers and then determine how they differ from their competitors. This strategy in turn helps customers understand how the particular company is unique and why its products or services should be preferred.

Creating Competitive Advantages

An organization has a competitive advantage when its customers perceive the company as better than its competitors. It has a competitive disadvantage when customers see the opposite: The company is perceived as inferior. When companies are similar in perceived performance, it's called "parity."

Consider an organization in which quality, service, and cost are all at parity with the competitors. No company appears to be better than the others. But if the company suffers a competitive disadvantage in innovation, what will happen if the company improves in innovation? Unless the change is substantial, all factors will remain at parity from the customer's perspective. The company will still have no clear competitive advantage. One way to achieve a competitive advantage is to focus attention on one condition already at parity with competitors—whether in quality, service, cost, innovation, or some other factor—and then maintain parity in the other factors.

A paper company had two strong strategic thrusts: cost and quality. When the company president was asked which was more important, he said, "Both!" Whenever the employees made decisions, they had to struggle to find a way to simultaneously improve quality and reduce costs. As a result, the company made many inconsistent decisions. Sometimes quality would win out and sometimes cost would, but the inconsistency cost the company energy.

A marketing study, conducted with a strategic-alignment survey, showed that the marketplace valued low cost over high quality. Customers would buy lower-cost paper if the quality was "good enough," but they would not purchase high-quality paper with higher prices. Thus, quality needed to be at parity with competitors. Once the company understood the tradeoff, this clarification of strategy helped drive the organization forward to gain a competitive advantage. Every person in the company was empowered to make decisions every day. For instance, a mill mechanic could make cost/quality decisions: He could install a new machine, but that would increase costs. So he would consider whether the existing machine placed quality at a competitive disadvantage or whether it maintained parity. When this level of strategic thought exists throughout an organization, competitors will have a difficult time regaining control of the market. The ability to distinguish between what's critical and what's important is what sets effective organizations apart from mediocre ones.[2]

Frontline employees in a large research and development company were asked to rank seven critical issues and processes by what they perceived as most important to managers. Paired comparisons were used to evaluate the feedback. For example, "What's more important: safety or controlling costs?" Safety was ranked above each of the other issues 100 percent of the time. The second most important issue to managers was cost efficiency, followed by keeping schedules, quantity of work, customer service, quality, and, finally, innovation.

Next, the R&D professionals in the same division were asked to make their own ranking. Their responses were remarkably similar in many ways: Safety was most important, followed by cost efficiency, customer service, quantity of work, innovation, keeping schedules, and quality.

Nothing seemed unusual about the data. But what was the message from managers about what's important? "Be safe and don't go over your budget. When we give you something, crank it out on time. Stay busy, provide good customer service, and if you need something to do, then you might want to work on quality and innovation." But what sort of message is that to send to employees responsible for quality and innovation? The survey showed that the employees and R&D professionals had been well-managed and efficient, but no breakthroughs ever occurred. A clear organizational focus helps companies determine what's most important.

The critical difference between the best companies and mediocre ones is that the best companies maintain world-class capability in a few critical areas while they execute other processes at parity with their competitors. In the meantime, mediocre organizations lack focus. They attempt to execute all processes at a world-class level. Too often, however, this lack of focus results in falling below parity with competitors in key areas, and it becomes impossible to achieve a competitive advantage.

Deciding What's Most Important

Whatever is measured will receive the attention of management. It can either distract the organization, or drive improvement and provide information to employees about what is important. If too many things are measured, or if the things measured do not lead to a competitive advantage, then both management and employees will be distracted. But if management focuses on one issue as a competitive advantage while maintaining parity on other essential issues, it will help the organization focus. The difficulty is in deciding what to measure because everything seems important. People have difficulty saying, "*A* is important, but *B* is not."

Most companies, at one time or another, have conducted some form of organizational assessment. Many of these assessments are not linked to the strategic direction of the company. Some measure happiness, while others measure skills, behaviors, or issues generally considered important. Review the following list and identify the items that are unimportant:

- Job satisfaction
- Good communication
- Efficient systems
- Effective supervision
- Ethics and honesty
- Flexibility
- Trust
- Quality
- Commitment to values
- Integrity
- Customer service
- Pride
- Innovation
- Collaboration between groups
- Teamwork
- Individual responsibility for work
- Good training and development
- Excellent recruiting
- Regular performance feedback
- Coaching
- Recognition of good work
- Rewards for high performance
- Top management leadership
- Technical competence
- Clear priorities
- Customer orientation
- Empowerment
- Employee commitment
- Involvement in decisions

At face value, most of the issues seem important. No one denies that most of these issues are valid, but attempting to perform all of them extremely well sends a complex and confusing message to the company. As a test, select eight to ten issues that, if done well, would directly implement or reinforce the strategic direction of your company. By doing this, you will have greater clarity about your strategy. If you can't complete the exercise quickly, then others in your company are probably paying as much attention to one item on the list as another.

One reason surveys aren't often linked to corporate strategy is because many companies aren't clear enough about their strategies to communicate implementation. Although they typically are crystal clear about desired outcomes (profits, growth), they cannot decide how best to achieve those outcomes. Organizations with low strategic clarity have difficulty narrowing their focus to a few essential issues. Figure 1.2 demonstrates the 80/20 principle of alignment: 80 percent of the business outcomes come from only 20 percent of the drivers of organizational effectiveness.

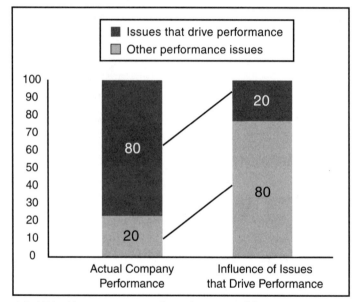

Figure 1.2: 80% of business outcomes derive from 20% of drivers.

Not every issue is critical for your organization's performance. Thus, assessments that measure the wrong things may distract the organization from doing critical work. In some organizations, management raises so many banners for new programs that employees have no sense of priority about what issues are more critical or important than others. In one organization, for example, managers would joke about giving the CEO a pile of internal reports and other documents to read whenever he went on a business trip. They wanted to "keep him from reading any books or magazines. Every time he reads a new magazine he comes back and implements a new program." A flurry of activity would occur when he returned, and then the initiatives would slowly be forgotten.

When using the 80/20 principle to assess issues that have high impact, be sure to evaluate not only what creates the impact, but also why it has impact.

For example, competency studies are often designed to solve the problem of deciding which skills are most important. These studies compare the most competent people with average people to determine what differentiates them.

In a study conducted for a major retailer, one skill was found that clearly differentiated high performers from average performers at the store level: Effective store managers paid attention to detail and focused on incremental improvements. Since this skill was found to differentiate high and average performers, would it create a competitive advantage if it were implemented chainwide? Perhaps. But, if the only reason store managers needed this skill was because systems were so bad they needed to pay attention to every detail to run a store efficiently, then training in the skill would be counterproductive. On the other hand, if competitors were to create a simple system that allowed managers to pay more attention to customers and employees, then attention to detail would not be as important as acquiring the new technology. In the end, management felt that if its competitors had similar systems, processes, and cultures, then improving this skill chainwide would indeed create a substantial advantage.

Designing Surveys for Competitive Advantage

The steps for designing surveys that measure alignment include:

1. Clarify strategy and implementation plans. The process begins with clarity about the company's strategy and the desired future of the organization. To do this, organizations must understand their competitors' strengths and weaknesses. Customer perceptions can be very insightful. Also, analyzing the best practices of similar organizations can provide clarity about which skills and technologies are necessary for implementing the strategy. Then the strategy needs to be operationalized. This means establishing a game plan for executing the strategy and determining what structures, systems, processes, and staff will be necessary.

2. Identify critical skills, competencies, characteristics, and behaviors for achieving the strategy. Once the company is clear about its strategy and that of its competitors, and has formulated an implementation plan, the next step requires identifying the tools needed to carry out the strategy. Evaluate which things the company must do better than its competitors and which things must be done as well as competitors. Some organizational skills and competencies may be necessary but do not need to be assessed because they are good enough. The company must measure only a few critical skills, characteristics, competencies, or behaviors and decide which things, if done extraordinarily well, will create the most market leverage.

3. Create measurement tools to assess effectiveness. Once the organizational skills, competencies, characteristics, or behaviors have been identified, create measurement tools to evaluate these areas. The assessment tool needs to assess each issue in the language of the company. Standard tools rarely accomplish this task. An assessment tool is not only an evaluation device, but a communication tool, and survey items often describe a desirable future state and help employees to envision that state.

4. Gather data and determine misalignments. Once the measurement tool has been selected or created, the survey may be administered. Misalignments can be determined in several ways:

• *Use tradeoff analysis to verify misalignment.* A large manufacturing company's strategic focus was quality, but it had recently encountered considerable cost pressure. When asked which one was more important, cost or quality, most managers and supervisors chose quality, but the employees in production chose cost. The message to production workers was, "If it costs more, don't do it!"

• *Refine strategic clarity.* Most survey efforts work on improving the most negative survey results, but organizations with a clear strategic focus use surveys to determine whether results ought to be more positive or negative. A foods company known for its innovation found its survey results for innovation to be good, but not good enough. Managers designed action plans to significantly improve innovation. They clearly understood that improvement in innovation would lead to a competitive advantage.

Strategic clarity may also help companies avoid focusing on issues that may appear slightly negative while the results are on parity with others or with norms. An executive of a high-tech company commented, "We should focus our efforts on improving collaboration between our divisions. But in terms of work-life balance, we are the same as our competitors."

• *Identify high and low groups.* Compare and contrast the groups to determine what misalignments caused the low groups to have problems and how the high groups were able to stay focused on company strategy.

5. Focus efforts to create the most leverage. Focusing change efforts to improve the few misalignments will create the greatest leverage for the organization. When strategy is clear, the change process works at both organizational and work group levels, all the way to the front lines. Each group can easily identify misalignments in their group and focus on them. Some misalignments may be the basis for companywide efforts, while others may be handled at the individual level.

Aligning Company Initiatives with Strategy

I have tried to show why companies should avoid tackling issues that are not linked to the strategy or to improving productivity and efficiency. Many may consider this advice to be crass and uncaring and ask, "What about changing significant social issues and improving people's lives—not because it benefits the bottom line, but because it is the right thing to do?"

My experience with companies trying to generate change on "good" issues not connected to their business strategy or bottom line is that, inevitably, those efforts fail. For example, many companies in the United States are trying to improve their cultures of diversity. Those who find ways to link the diversity issue to their business strategy have always been more successful in making real change occur than those who do it because it was "the right thing to do." Those companies that value being "a good neighbor" and that find ways to link that concept with their corporate strategy, tend to experience greater success. The following cases further demonstrate this point:

(Scenario 1) The top management team in Company A decided to hire twenty-five employees per year who had previously been on welfare. The announcement was made quoting one of the company's values: "We believe in being a good neighbor in the communities where we operate." In the opinion of many employees, the announcement made the move seem like an act of charity. The human resources department received a quota, along with the message that "twenty-five former welfare recipients better be working in the company by the end of the year."

As a result of the effort, twenty-five people who had formerly been on welfare were offered jobs that year, and managers were given the implicit message that these people were "protected." Most of the new recruits showed very poor job performance but were rarely disciplined. At year's end the twenty-five people were still employed, but their peers had become angry. Some had even lowered their performance standards to be in line with the performance of the new employees.

(Scenario 2) The top management team in Company B also decided to hire twenty-five employees per year who had previously been on welfare. The announcement said that the company believed these people could be excellent employees and would have high standards of performance. Top management communicated that, to succeed, these employees would need two things: (1) a chance to succeed, and (2) a coach or mentor to show them the ropes. The company selected twenty-five employees to be trained as coaches or mentors for the new employees.

As the new employees were hired, they received a great deal of attention and help, but they received no special treatment. Unauthorized absences and tardiness were not tolerated. Poor performance was reviewed promptly with the new employees. Several soon quit, and a few others were fired. But the majority of the former welfare recipients eventually became excellent examples and some of the most dependable employees in the company.

The difference in these two scenarios is that in scenario 1, Company A tried to do "the right thing" regardless of the impact it would have on the business. But in scenario 2, Company B did the right thing and also helped the business become more successful.

I encourage companies to be generous and helpful in the community, and to participate in volunteerism and other acts of charity. But these efforts work best when they are linked to the mission and purpose of the company. Initiatives that attempt to solve social or individual problems but do not contribute to the long-term success of the company end up being demoralizing distractions. Their drain on the company is often a cue to employees that high performance and excellence are not important.

Employee surveys can have a dramatic impact on the effectiveness of an organization. In order for these positive outcomes to be achieved, however, survey questions, processes, and feedback must be balanced against the expectations they generate. Successful employee surveys achieve balance. Unsuccessful surveys generate impossibly high expectations.

In the past few years, strategic alignment has become a very popular term. And although it may be nice to talk about, it is even better to measure. Measuring alignment with employee surveys not only helps determine whether companies are aligned with their strategies, but can also be used to improve alignment and focus, as well as to identify competitive advantages.

Notes to Chapter One

1. Thomas J. Peters and Robert H. Waterman, *In Search of Excellence*. New York: Harper & Row, 1982, 16.

2. For an interesting look at strategy, read Lee Tom Perry, Randall G. Stott, and W. Norman Smallwood, *Real-Time Strategy: Improvising Team-Based Planning for a Fast-Changing World*. New York: Wiley & Sons, 1993, 97-122.

CHAPTER TWO

Three Approaches to Surveys

In over 20 years of designing and conducting organizational surveys, I have often met managers who complain that the idea behind surveys is "right," but that the results often do not justify the effort. Many companies have had a good first experience with surveys, but follow-up surveys do not produce new information. Further, employees soon get tired of "filling out forms" that don't lead to desired changes.

The most common problem behind these complaints is that surveys designed to accomplish a specific purpose (often purchased "off-the-shelf") are usually adapted to suit every purpose. But we can't expect to use surveys designed for one use, such as gathering information on employee satisfaction, to help in another use, such as measuring the implementation of new policies or determining the alignment of company strategies. Similarly, most companies don't need to conduct comprehensive surveys to have a successful survey experience. Before any survey is used, companies should first communicate the specific uses and objectives of the survey to participants.

Three different approaches to surveys can help organizations narrow their search and more effectively find the information they need.

- Gathering information
- Implementing changes
- Aligning strategies

Gathering Information

Surveys designed to gather information are the most common. Most surveys developed by companies for internal use (without the help of consultants), and many of the surveys designed for so-called "off-the-shelf" purchase from training and development firms, have this objective. This approach typically involves administering a standardized survey to sample groups of employees to determine their perceptions about company policies and practices. The information is used to make decisions on company policies, most often human resource polices.

The information-gathering approach, also called the "temperature-taking" approach (because it is used only to check the general climate of attitudes), has several limitations. First, surveys designed to gather information should only be used occasionally, perhaps once every five years. Without significant changes to policies as a result of the survey, employees may feel that management is refusing to act on their feedback. Second, such surveys work best when administered only to small samples of employees. Surveys designed to reveal employee opinions ought to remain subtle and unobtrusive, rather than become major events and productions. If these limitations are exceeded, companies risk raising or violating employee expectations.

The president of a large public utility wanted to gather information on how employees felt about working conditions. Senior management contracted a well-known survey firm to conduct the survey, which selected a statistically valid sample of 100 employees to participate. The firm administered the survey, analyzed the results, and reported to senior management, which used the information to improve human resource policies. But the results were never shared with the participants in the sample or with employees in general.

Two years later, another survey firm conducted a follow-up survey. Prior to administering the survey, the firm interviewed 50 employees, who expressed frustrations about the prospect of completing another survey. They reported that conditions were worse as a result of the last survey, saying, "Why weren't we involved the last time?" "The results must have been negative, because if they had been positive they would have told us." "This is a management tool to get rid of supervisors who aren't performing. One supervisor was fired two months after the last survey." "Managers are just whitewashing this whole thing."

In this company, the survey process actually created dissatisfaction. Instead of simply gathering information or determining employee opinions, the survey created unanticipated expectations for changes that never occurred.

To avoid potential problems when using surveys designed to gather information, make sure you:

1. Clearly state the objectives of the survey to participants. If the objectives are not clearly communicated up front, then employees may overestimate the actions that will result from the feedback.[1]

2. Understand why certain technical methods were used in designing the survey. For example, sophisticated sampling methods and statistical procedures can be drawbacks if it appears management is trying to "hide something" or "get the results it wants." In the case of the utility company, employees could not understand why only a few people participated. Similarly, people tend to agree with the concept of sampling until they disagree with the results. When this happens, they often argue that their group or department is unique and should be treated differently.

3. Share the results with survey participants. Often, managers believe that it's better for morale to keep the results of a survey confidential. But in practice, it's impossible to avoid communicating the results. In fact, if the results are not shared, employees tend to assume the results on their own. In the utility company example, the firing of a supervisor was linked to the survey by employees who were attempting to make sense of several unrelated events. The survey became a convenient scapegoat.

Generally, the actual results of a survey are rarely as bad as the rumors created when results are not communicated. While you don't necessarily want the results of information-gathering surveys to be published for everyone, the people who actually take the surveys will likely communicate with their peers. Make sure they know why they are taking the survey when they take it, and what the results were after they complete it.

4. Use surveys for the specific purposes for which they are designed. Many organizations conduct employee surveys with the intent to gather information—and use a survey that is appropriate for such use. But, after gathering the information and finding several areas in need of change, managers often transform the purpose of the survey to implement changes. Changing from one approach to another is rarely successful. If changes are to result from the survey process, then employees should be involved from the beginning, and a survey designed to implement changes should be used.

Figure 2.1 outlines a typical process flow for using a survey to gather information.

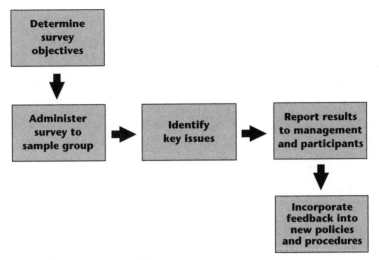

Figure 2.1: Typical process for doing a survey.

Implementing Changes

The change-implementation approach can add significant value to the information-gathering approach. While
the information-gathering approach is often referred to as
the "temperature-taking" approach because of its limitations, the change-implementing approach is designed to
make effective organizational improvements. Rather than
using standardized questionnaires, the survey questions are
customized to each department or group. Everyone in each
department or group is surveyed to determine the most pertinent issues to address in making changes. The results are
used not only by managers, but also by employees in group
feedback sessions. Figure 2.2 outlines a typical process flow
for using a survey to implement changes.

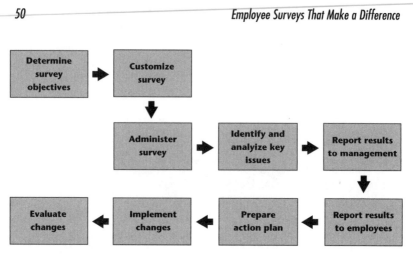

Figure 2.2: Typical process for implementing changes from a survey.

Four major differences between using surveys to gather information and using them to implement change include:

1. *The change-implementation approach involves everyone in the change process.* By asking everyone's opinion before making changes that affect them, companies can increase the "buy-in" of employees. The simple act of gathering opinions generates energy for change.[2] And, when the time comes to make changes, it will be easier for employees to participate with management in solving problems and improving the company.

The CEO of a large government contractor recently reviewed the data from his company survey and commented, "Top management can only impact two or three of the ten highest-priority issues. I want to be sure the managers responsible for the other eight issues see this information and commit to making changes where necessary." Rather than hiding the negative results, the CEO properly delegated the responsibility for decision-making to the managers. Changes would not have occurred as quickly in this company if the CEO had assumed responsibility for all the problems. He was able to bring about changes by fostering internal commitment, an essential component of empowerment.[3]

2. Employees participate more readily when they are involved in making changes. To illustrate this, consider the influence of the Nielsen rating system on television programming. Nielsen ratings are determined by sampling the viewing habits of "typical" American families. Whenever a show is canceled, viewers who liked the show typically blame the "dumb" families in the sample who "obviously" had no taste. Similarly, employees tend to discount survey feedback when they have not contributed to it.

In implementing changes, small sample sizes can lead to hostility in the change process.[4] Differences between work groups are often striking, and it would be difficult to convince one department's employees to make changes based on another department's survey, or even based on a total-company survey. Such broad-brush action is often inappropriate. Instead, changes in a department should be based on feedback obtained from that department (unless a survey is designed for aligning company strategy, which will be discussed later on).

3. Customized surveys improve accuracy, increase the relevance to particular groups or departments, and foster ownership of the change process by employees. Unlike the information-gathering approach, where standardized tests help managers shape company policies, the change-implementation approach (though it may include some standardized questions) includes customized questions for each department or group. The customized questions assess specific issues not covered in standard surveys. Effective customization will change how employees perceive the survey from "their survey" to "our survey."

4. Employee feedback sessions are an important, but sensitive, part of the change process. Skeptical employees wonder if their comments and perceptions will be "soft-pedaled," or even censored. Managers don't want to embarrass supervisors who receive negative survey feedback, nor do they want to inadvertently give feedback that might harm someone's credibility. If feedback sessions are managed properly, they may be used to clarify what the employees intended to communicate in their survey responses.[5] For example, one comment from a survey read, "I receive no feedback whatsoever. I don't know if I'm in line for chairman of the board or the unemployment line." In a feedback session, a clever facilitator can use this comment to generate a fun, yet useful dialogue for improving communication in the company.

Companies that successfully use the change-implementation approach begin by communicating their objectives up front, and then follow through by drawing appropriate conclusions from the survey results and involving employees in making changes.

A drawback to the change approach is that employees often perceive surveys to be the domain of the human resources department. This may occur if too many questions are asked regarding company policies or employee benefits. Although these may be important issues, if surveys are not perceived by employees as critical to the business, they lose relevance and become counterproductive.

The vice-president of human resources of a Midwestern engineering company was feeling discouraged. Her department had surveyed each department in the company every 18 months for the past four years. But administering the survey to employees, analyzing the information, and then reporting to management and employee groups had definitely lost its luster.

Initially, everyone had been excited about responding to survey questions regarding how they perceived the organization and what could be done to improve effectiveness. Lately, however, she felt that she was no longer facilitating the process—she was driving it. Line managers who initially had responded enthusiastically now referred to the survey as part of "company bureaucracy" or, even worse, "HR bureaucracy." This was not what she had envisioned. But, once she realized she had been mixing the information-gathering approach and the change-implementation approach, she was able to set clear objectives. In fact, she determined that the strategic-alignment approach was best for her situation.

Aligning Strategy

The strategic-alignment approach involves both line managers and human resources personnel in making organizational improvements that impact the strategic direction of the company. It is a total organizational approach aimed at determining gaps between where the company is and where it wants to go. Strategic alignment surveys tend to be received more enthusiastically by employees. While information-gathering surveys are designed in the language of research and analysis and change-implementation surveys are designed for specific departments, strategic-alignment surveys are designed in the language of the organization. They feel like, look like, and sound like the company (rather than a research project or human resources exercise), and employees see more direct correlation between the survey and the issues faced by the company. Figure 2.3 outlines a typical process flow for using a survey to align company strategy.

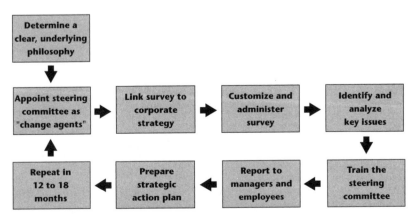

Figure 2.3: Typical process strategic alignment approach to surveys.

The underlying philosophy. The success of the strategic-alignment approach depends on the company's strategic philosophy. Companies that have had success with this approach have incorporated the survey process as an ongoing part of how they do business. The survey becomes less of an "event" and more of an ongoing change catalyst. Other keys to success with this approach include:

- Recognize that the process (how and when the survey is administered and who is involved) is as important as the content (what is asked and how the information is analyzed).
- Survey whole departments or groups rather than sampling demographic groups.
- Involve employee groups in assessing, planning, and implementing strategies.
- Repeat the survey every 12 to 18 months.

Rather than measuring employee satisfaction, strategic-alignment surveys are designed to measure the key issues that impact a company's strategy. While the other two approaches "take a temperature" or obtain information relevant only to specific departments, they do not generally lead to changes that make the company more competitive, and both managers and employees often do not see the correlation between the surveys and the day-to-day problems they face at work. Without this correlation, both groups perceive surveys as distractions from the real work of the organization. When surveys do not help with strategic issues, critics often ask, "Are happy employees more productive?" They do not see how the survey feedback would lead to competitive advantages such as higher productivity or improved effectiveness.

For many years, before it became fashionable, a large manufacturing company had posted its values statement in the lobby. One day, the vice president of human resources decided that, rather than use a survey with standardized questions, he would perform a "values audit" to see if employees felt the company was "walking its talk."

Initially, senior management merely approved the survey to "measure the attitudes" of employees at the corporate offices, but, as time passed, the senior managers and the CEO became more interested and involved, requesting weekly updates. "Living the values" was considered key to company culture, and the culture was perceived as critical to company success worldwide.

Information about the culture that came from the "values audit" was determined to be indispensable to senior management, and the survey provided a vehicle to operationalize the company's values statement. The process proved to be so successful at the corporate offices that managers at every location were invited to participate. It turned out that those managers had always understood the link between "living the values" and succeeding competitively, and felt the values helped customers differentiate between the company and its competitors.

Perhaps the best way to make sure adequate attention is paid to strategic issues is to schedule periodic surveys. People tend to pay attention to what is measured, and measuring only once signals that the company is merely curious, not committed. Measuring on a regular basis indicates that the issues are critical and ought to be improved.

The steering committee "change agents." The human resources vice-president referred to earlier described how she felt she had been "driving the process" instead of facilitating it. This happens when (1) line managers lose interest, or (2) the human resources department changes policies without involving those affected. (Lack of interest is more common.)

The strategic-alignment approach links the survey to the business vision, and involves both line managers and a human resources manager. The "steering committee" helps foster that link and may include up to twelve participants from different parts of the company. The committee's role is to facilitate the change process in the company or department.[6] This committee may create separate task forces, perhaps involving employees outside the steering committee, to work on targeted issues, but the steering committee should not be disbanded until a new survey is conducted. Since managed change rarely occurs without responsibility, this small group—which channels that responsibility and is trained in dealing with potential problems—is critical to the success of this approach. (I will cover steering committees in greater detail in Chapter 5.)

Linking surveys to corporate strategy. While the information-gathering approach compares survey results to national norms and the change-implementation approach uses both national norms and targets specific departments, the most significant benefit of the strategic-alignment approach is the additional ability to compare the organization's strengths and weaknesses to itself in an ideal or desired future state.

Organizations must constantly change and adapt. Using the information-gathering or change-implementation approaches to align company strategy can cause several problems.

Typically, these surveys present data as a picture of the company's strengths and weaknesses, under the assumption that if the company would simply recognize its weaknesses and make changes, the weaknesses would turn into strengths and then, if the company continued to address its weaknesses, it would eventually have none. In response to this picture, the weakest issues are worked on first until they are resolved. Then, when those are "fixed," the next weakest are worked on, and so forth. The underlying belief is that in ten or fifteen or twenty years, everything will be perfect. But, because the external environment constantly shifts, as competition, market demands, and other factors force new issues to the table, these methods will never lead to competitive advantages. Management must pay attention to different variables each year as competition shifts.

The strategic-alignment approach embraces a more realistic view: that tradeoffs are inherent in organizational life. This view helps managers recognize which key factors must be executed better than competitors and which should be done as well as competitors. The strategic vision of the company then determines which tradeoffs should be made.

For example, a manufacturing company's mission was to "deliver what the customer orders on time with high quality." When top managers were questioned about the appropriateness of introducing a new product in a different market, making it impossible to fulfill orders on time in their core business, the group recognized it had made an incorrect tradeoff. It had focused too many resources on a new, unproven product while their core products suffered. Companies should have an explicit statement of their strategies (vision statements), and strategic-alignment surveys should be linked to these statements. Once the mission is clear, a survey may be used to operationalize the behaviors, attitudes, structures, products and services, and tasks that are critical to success.

Customizing according to strategy. Instead of thinking up what to ask, or asking strictly satisfaction-type questions, the steering committee determines the issues that are most pertinent to the company and designs the questions accordingly. In the manufacturing company just mentioned, the steering committee formulated a number of customized questions based on speed and quality issues. The focus should now turn to measuring the gap between where the organization currently is and where it needs to go. Now that the questions are business-related, the importance of the entire effort is elevated. In the information-gathering approach, the vice-president of human resources heard comments about "company and HR bureaucracy." In the strategic approach, responses to the questions become a vital part of the strategic planning process. Measuring progress regularly, perhaps every 18-24 months, becomes a necessity. The survey becomes part of the stewardship and accountability process.

Training the steering committee. A common cause of failure in information-gathering and change-implementation approaches is that training rarely follows the survey. Even when participants are enthusiastic about making changes, they don't often know where to begin. By training the steering committee, companies can increase their leverage in accomplishing several objectives. First, if the steering committee represents the key line managers and the human resources department, then training the committee increases the likelihood of change in their respective groups. Second, if the steering committee has a common framework to draw upon, supplied by training, that framework can help the committee determine which areas in the company, department, team, or demographic group to focus on to achieve the greatest impact. Third, training the steering committee renews the committee members' commitment and provides a logical next step for action.

The president of a medium-sized computer company took his company's steering committee to an off-site location for training in the key areas identified by a strategic-alignment survey, inviting outside experts along to help with the three highest-priority issues. The three-day workshop was an unqualified success. And, because the survey had been customized according to the company's strategic direction, the facilitators had little problem identifying key issues. The offsite location provided an opportunity to focus on the future of the company without interruption.

One senior vice-president said it was the first "strategic training" he had received.

Content of training. Once the decision should be made to train the steering committee, the next decision is to determine the content of that training. The steering committee should be trained to work on the most important issues identified by the survey. Typically, companies at this point assume that the most negative items demand the most attention. In one case, a large hotel and restaurant company contracted with an outside consulting firm to conduct an employee survey. When the results came in, the most negative concern was that employees felt they needed a pay increase. Even though the raise was expensive, management granted an 8 percent salary increase across the board, in addition to the annual performance increase.

Two years later another survey was conducted, and, once again, the most negative issue was pay. But this time, instead of focusing on the most negative issues, the steering committee had been trained to identify which survey items best predicted overall company effectiveness. This revealed that the predominant issue was not in fact pay, but that employees lacked feedback on their performance from supervisors. By training the supervisors to provide clearer and more frequent feedback, the company as a whole became more effective.

Most negative versus highest impact concerns. Frederick Herzberg's theory of motivation states that motivation is governed by "hygiene factors" and "motivators." And, although most basic courses in management cover this theory, most employee surveys ignore it. "Motivators," organizational practices that motivate people, are intrinsically satisfying. They include such things as pride in quality work, recognition or rewards for a job well-done, and the hope that promotions will follow continued success over time. Herzberg also argues that increasing the motivators in a job increase employee motivation. "Hygiene factors" are an employee's conditions of ongoing employment, such as pay, working conditions, benefits, hours, and company policies. Improving hygiene factors does not necessarily increase motivation.[7]

When surveys concentrate on the most negative areas, they often measure only hygiene factors. Employees often complain about hygiene factors even when those are equitable, but such complaints are often symptomatic of other concerns. For example, if employees feel their pay is fair but don't like the department supervisor, then they tend to reason that a raise is merited because they have to tolerate the situation. If their pay is, in fact, low, then it would be a mistake for management not to increase it, but if pay is not a high-impact concern, then money and attention will not solve the problem and the more important concern will remain.

Surveys that differentiate between "most negative" and "highest impact" concerns are very effective in helping companies profit from their investment in the surveys. By training the steering committee, companies can not only identify but also resolve high-impact concerns more effectively.

The feedback session. Companies that use information-gathering and change-implementation approaches often have a human resources manager present the feedback to managers and employees. But in the strategic-alignment approach, the human resources manager may only act as a consultant to the steering committee, giving only part—if any—of the feedback. Members of the steering committee who have been trained to understand the survey will have strong ideas for action and can make the most effective presentations to their own departments. This increases the likelihood that the steering committee will act on the highest impact areas.

Also, rather than approaching feedback sessions as simple reports or presentations, the best approach is to present

survey feedback as a stimulus for dialogue in which everyone commits to participate in making improvements. For
example, if a survey reveals many negative comments about
a lack of information regarding the company's future, it
would be useful to find out what information the employees want and why they feel they need it. The most vocal or
popular employees might be asked to participate in a task
force or study group to make further recommendations.

The research and development manager of a large oil company reviewed his survey results. Much of the feedback made
sense, but one comment stood out. It said he was "unavail-
able and aloof." This surprised him because he'd always had
an open-door policy. He thought his employees could visit
him whenever they wished. He decided to schedule a meeting
to discuss the feedback with his staff. In the meeting he told
the group he had been surprised by the feedback and then
asked for clarification. One of the employees asked, "You
mean you don't know? Ever since you hired that new secretary she has controlled who sees you and when they can see
you. She's like a guard: If she doesn't want to let you in, you
don't get in." Having clarified the feedback, the manager was
able to train his secretary on his open-door policy.

The strategic action plan. When the results of a survey
are compared to the company's future vision, key gaps
between present and future become evident. First, one
compares the present configuration of strengths and weaknesses with the desired configuration. The most nega-
tive/highest impact issues that appear in the delta of
present and desired states become the key issues for organizational improvement efforts. Improving these issues
becomes a high priority because they are the high-impact
organizational areas that stand in the way of the organization fulfilling its vision and strategy. It is hard to imagine
senior management not allocating resources to these areas,
for they are critical to organizational success.

Summary

Information-gathering, change-implementation, and strategic-alignment approaches have distinct purposes and may all be implemented successfully. However, because of its limitations, the information-gathering approach should be used infrequently because enthusiasm for this approach invariably wanes over time and expectations are frequently violated.

The change-implementation approach is an interim step between information gathering and strategic alignment. Before moving to a strategic-alignment approach, the change-implementation approach may be used to build credibility and to familiarize managers with using surveys effectively.

The strategic-alignment approach yields the most leverage. Surveys are a vital force for improvement when they are integrated into how the company does business, and they help determine steps of action for achieving the future vision.

Thinking through what is really wanted from the survey, communicating these expectations clearly, and then managing the process make the difference between successful and unsuccessful survey efforts. The results can make a significant contribution to how a company manages its people, uses its resources, and achieves its vision.

To the extent that organizations can create strategic approaches, their survey efforts will be more successful and endure through time. The strategic-alignment approach guarantees that the issues addressed are linked to the company's strategy. Strategic surveys capture the energy and commitment of both managers and employees. They send a consistent message because they focus on issues that top management constantly talks about. In well-constructed strategic-alignment surveys, employees can see the connection between the survey and desired outcomes. Managers and executives have higher commitment to change because the issues are more likely to lead to organizational success.

Notes to Chapter Two

1. Tom Salemme, "Look Before You Leap." *HR Focus* 72 (January 1995). 7.

2. David A. Nadler, *Feedback and Organization Development: Using Data-Based Methods*. Reading, MA: Addison-Wesley, 1977, 59.

3. Chris Argyris, "Empowerment: The Emperor's New Clothes." *Harvard Business Review*. May-June 1998, 100.

4. Jack E. Edwards, Marie D. Thomas, Paul Rosenfeld, and Booth Kewle. *How to Conduct Organizational Surveys: A Step-by-Step Guide*. Thousand Oaks, CA: Sage Publications, 1997, 64.

5. Randall Dunham and Frank Smith, *Organizational Surveys: An Internal Assessment of Organizational Health*. Glenview, IL: Scott, Foresman, 1979, 121.

6. Allen I. Kraut, "Organizational Research on Work and Family Issues" in Sheldon Zedeck, ed., *Work, Families, and Organizations*. San Francisco, CA: Jossey-Bass, 1992, 208-35.

7. Frederick Herzberg, Bernard Mausner, and Barbara Bloch Snyderman, *The Motivation to Work*. New York: Wiley & Sons, 1959.

CHAPTER THREE

The Right Time for an Employee Survey

The vice-president of human resources for a large manufacturing company was preparing to conduct an employee survey. Five weeks before she administered the survey, she was called into an emergency meeting and told that the company would be cutting its staff by ten percent in two weeks. The company president was concerned about the timing, and he asked the vice president whether the company should administer the survey as planned, or delay it.

Such scenarios are occurring with increasing frequency. Many organizations respond by delaying their surveys, hoping things will settle down. Unfortunately, in today's turbulent business environment, things don't always work out that way: six-month delays stretch to a year, two years, and so on.

For example, one company completed the initial planning for an employee survey and then postponed it. Management reconsidered conducting the survey in subsequent years but was always concerned about a possible reorganization, a reduction in orders, an acquisition, or a move to a new location. Each year, managers agreed that the survey ought to be conducted every year, but then decided to delay the survey until the following year, when things would be "back to normal." This happened over a period of five years, until, ultimately, the managers stopped having meetings to discuss surveys.

Reasons to Delay

Typically, executives worry that survey results will be more negative because of a major event, and so they postpone or cancel their surveys. They feel the results may not accurately reflect the real attitudes of employees and that such events create tremendous bias.

Major reorganization: A good reason. Although there may be no perfect time to administer an employee survey, some times are better than others. Most of the time, it's best to press on despite less-than-optimal conditions. However, in the case above, downsizing one week and administering an employee survey the next might send a contradictory message to employees, especially if the survey is presented as, "the voice of the people." It may be wise to avoid the appearance of hypocrisy by postponing or canceling a survey immediately after a major reorganization, but this would not eliminate the need to conduct a survey sometime later to determine the impact of the change on productivity.

Managers must deal with two concurrent realities: (1) They must run efficient, effective, and profitable businesses, and (2) they must consider the welfare, morale, and success of their employees. Managers cannot sacrifice one reality for the other. If difficult conditions prompt you to delay a survey that your employees have been expecting, you could make a bad situation worse. Employees may draw their own conclusions: "I knew things were bad, but did you hear they just canceled the survey? The worst must be still to come." If you must delay a survey, make sure you communicate your reasons to employees.

Avoiding bad news: A bad reason. Some managers believe that challenging events will poison employee attitudes and cause employees to report that positive things are negative. This won't occur if surveys are constructed correctly and if the company maintains a healthy level of trust with its employees. Instead, adverse events significantly affect the way employees respond only to the survey items directly related to those events. In the above example, the layoff would greatly affect how employees respond to the item: "I expect to be laid off or transferred to a less desirable job." Research shows, however, that a layoff would not substantially affect items that address other working conditions such as supervision, pay, or career satisfaction.

In fact, when employee surveys place recent, stressful events in context, their feedback produces a valid measurement of employee attitudes. Managers may even soften the impact of unpleasant events by using surveys to face their situations squarely and by encouraging employees to provide feedback.

One company that used this approach introduced its survey by saying, "We've had a difficult year. Some of our friends and co-workers have lost their jobs, and we sincerely regret we had to lay off employees. But it is now time for us to regroup. We need to be more effective and efficient than ever, and to do this we need your help. We are asking for your views on many critical issues. Please respond to each item as honestly as possible, and help us understand what we can do to help move this organization forward."

Managers frequently subscribe to the premise that no news is good news, or at least that it's better than bad news. Consider the manager of a group of design engineers, for example. As part of a major reorganization, the group was recently cut by 50 percent, and the remaining engineers' jobs were changed significantly. The manager wanted things to cool down before embarking on an employee survey, reasoning, "The group is just too negative right now. The survey will only confirm how bad things are, and seeing the results will cause more problems because there isn't much I can do."

It takes courage to ask questions that might prompt unpleasant answers. Often, when we think things are bad, we avoid taking actions that might confirm our suspicions. Some managers conduct employee surveys only when they're sure the results will confirm that employees feel good about the company and morale is high, believing it's better to assume the worst than to find out the truth. But ignorance only leaves organizations in limbo.

If we ask the right questions, we may find out that things are not as bad as we expected. That's what the manager of the engineering designers discovered. He was persuaded to proceed with the survey despite his misgivings. To his surprise, the findings were much more positive than he had expected, and the company identified several issues he could address.

Surveys as Tools, Not Tests

Ultimately, the success of a survey does not rest on its findings—whether positive or negative—but on whether the findings serve as a springboard for improvement. If managers are held accountable for how positive or negative survey results are, with no consideration for the impact of recent events, they will manage the timing of surveys to ensure that the results will be as positive as possible. After all, it's in their best interest to do so. On the other hand, if managers are judged on what they do with the results, then they will be more amenable to conducting surveys in tough times.

To be sure his employee surveys served as a catalyst for change, the vice-president of human resources at a large food company addressed the issue as part of managers' performance evaluations. At this company, managers were not judged by the results of employee surveys, but by what they did with the results. A manager who received positive feedback from employees, but who then devised a slipshod strategy for maintaining the positive climate, would receive a poor evaluation. On the other hand, a manager who received negative feedback, but who came up with a strong action plan to turn things around, would receive a positive evaluation.

Sometimes managers receive feedback on issues they can't resolve. When this happens, managers should:

- Acknowledge employee feedback.
- Share concern for the issue.
- Acknowledge they can't change the issue.
- Ask for employee input on how best to cope with the situation.
- Select three other issues that can be changed, and take action on those.

Although there may be no perfect time to administer an employee survey, employees will respond to their surveys honestly, even in times of turmoil, if they have confidence that their feedback will spur positive change.[1] Managers who ask for feedback usually find that things are better than they expected. Additionally, they gather the information they need to resolve problems and move their organizations forward. If a survey is viewed as a tool to move an organization forward rather than as a test to see who gets the best score, the process always works well. Over the long run, using surveys as tools to move an organization forward will produce more positive outcomes.

Attitudes about Surveys

It is interesting how people think differently about some measures than others. For example, if a company has come upon hard financial times, would you ever imagine that the executives would resist reviewing the financial reports? No. In fact, the opposite usually occurs. When companies are struggling financially, they demand even more data. Likewise, if a manufacturing plant has been creating too much waste, would the managers resist reviewing reports on waste volume? Of course not. If a company had recently lost a large sale to a competitor, would salespeople resist learning the reason they lost the contract? Never. They would want to learn what went wrong so they could try to win similar contracts in the future.

What, then, is the rationale for executives to resist reviewing the results of employee surveys when negative feedback is involved? (In my twenty years of experience, I have never heard of a survey being canceled because of an overwhelmingly positive event.) The answer lies in how executives view surveys. Too often, they look to surveys as report cards, rather than as useful measurement tools to assist managers in running their business.

In a recent panel discussion, the question was asked, "How do you know if an organization is ready for a survey?" The experts quickly identified a list of conditions that would be optimal for a successful employee survey. But, as I reviewed the list, it became apparent that if such conditions existed, an organization would not need to conduct a survey because it would already be functioning effectively. I wondered: If an organization doesn't have these conditions, should it wait to conduct a survey? I proposed, "We have good evidence to suggest that organizations that conduct surveys have a competitive advantage over those who don't."

If you are not conducting regular employee surveys and your competitors are, you are at a disadvantage. Assuming their surveys are done correctly, your competitors are measuring critical factors that, if resolved, would make them more productive and efficient. Likewise, if your organization is not measuring those factors, then you are losing ground.

Suppose an organization finds a new production technique that would dramatically lower the costs of production. But, after looking closely at the technology, the company determines it does not have the skills to implement it. Should the company wait a few years to acquire the skills before using the technology? Probably not. Most organizations would move quickly to acquire the skills, because if they wait too long, they might find themselves out of business. Similarly, it would not make sense to acquire the technology and then let it sit idle. It would be important to implement the new technology as quickly as possible.

Employee surveys, when done well, have the potential to create substantial advantages for organizations. If your organization has been waiting for the right time, for optimal conditions, or for a more supportive climate, you may be creating disadvantages for your company.

So, When Is the Right Time?

When is the right time to conduct employee surveys? The answer is the same as for these other questions: When is it the right time to measure company profits? When is the right time to measure production efficiency? When is the right time to measure quality? The answer to all these questions is "as soon as additional information is needed to make an informed decision." Despite this importance, I find that many companies have an almost natural tendency to postpone their employee surveys.

When I examine my own life, I find this same tendency: I frequently find that the answer to "When is the right time to exercise?" is influenced by many good reasons (also known as excuses) such as "I'm tired," "My knee hurts," "I'm too busy today," or "It's too cold outside." The net result is less exercise. The problem is that I do not set a minimum standard. But if I set a standard, such as "I will exercise three times a week, no excuses," I would drive myself to keep the standard.

In organizations that maintain reasonable consistency in their employee surveys, an expectation is established about how often they should be conducted. This expectation is usually set by the executive who sets the precedent. Organizations that are inconsistent in conducting surveys see significant decline in the effectiveness of those surveys.

Here are three of the most popular options for companies that conduct regular surveys:

Yearly. Many organizations are committed to surveying once a year. To maintain such frequency, surveys need to be administered quickly and efficiently. The action plans need to be put in place as soon as possible after the survey. The drawback for yearly surveys is that sometimes that is too frequent. The action plans from one survey are not always implemented sufficiently to impact the survey of the following year.

Every 18 months. An 18-month cycle provides excellent timing to measure the implementation of changes in the company. The problem with this option is that many companies find it difficult to maintain the schedule as they switch from winter one year to summer the next, and so forth.

Every two years. Many companies prefer a two-year cycle. The problem is that sometimes this survey cycle is too long. It is difficult to maintain enthusiasm and focus on the process over two years. To help maintain the momentum, some companies have a two-year cycle with a mini-survey at the one-year mark to assess key action items.

Although it may make sense for companies to adjust their survey schedules because of major reorganizations, business crises, or other downturns, establishing and maintaining a consistent schedule for employee surveys can have a significant influence on driving positive organizational change.

Notes to Chapter Three

1. David A. Nadler, *Feedback and Organization Development: Using Data-based Methods*. Reading, MA: Addison-Wesley, 1977, 65.

CHAPTER FOUR

Tradeoffs in Survey Methods

A recent news article noted a trend in human behavior called "time stacking."[1] Time stackers are the sorts of people who call their clients on the way to a child's soccer match. Then, during the soccer match, they work on their day planners to plan the next day's activities while they watch the game.

When people become over-committed, time stacking helps them accomplish more; but it doesn't always work for relationships. For example, the children of time-stacking parents often notice the lack of attention from their parents, and the parents who time-stack often do not accomplish high-quality work. When my wife and I struggled with time stacking earlier in our marriage, one of my children developed the habit of placing both hands on my wife's face and holding her close while he communicated to her things he felt were important.

Behaviors such as time-stacking are the products of a culture that believes in "having it all." Busy executives believe they can be everything: high-impact leaders, great fathers and mothers, community leaders, active churchgoers, long-distance runners, and fly fishers. Perhaps they can, but not without a price.

In organizations, this same philosophy of having it all has assumed the form of "doing more with less." We cut our staffs by 25 percent while we try to increase our sales by 50 percent. This approach, on both the personal and organizational levels, has led to many great successes, but it has also driven people and companies to dead ends, and often to burnouts or breakdowns.

Tradeoffs

Life is full of tradeoffs. One of my father's favorite quotes was, "If you dance, you've got to pay the fiddler." I usually heard that line on a Saturday morning as he would awaken me from sleep after I had stayed out late on a Friday night. My attitude in those years was that I was invincible: I thought I could stay out late and still get up on time and work hard. But those mornings were never as easy as I had planned.

Although I found that I could stay out late and forego some sleep, eventually fatigue would catch up with me. Soon, sleep would become more important than hanging out late with my friends. As I got older, I came to appreciate my father's advice. He understood the concept of tradeoffs: If you choose option *A*, it will affect option *B*. I had been lucky that a lack of sleep never caused me to get fired or to fall asleep while driving.

I think many managers have experienced a similar "invincible" attitude. For example, many leaders say, "I want high profitability, a low head count, and high morale." Such bold visions encourage people to make their best efforts to help build a profitable company. These goals are admirable and often possible with exceptional efforts from a few trusted workers. But real tradeoffs will eventually take their effects: "If you dance, you've got to pay the fiddler." In the same way that I would become worn out and tired after staying out too late, people in business begin to wear down under the weight of excessive work. Any activity achieved though sheer force or effort alone cannot be maintained for long.

Employee surveys are loaded with tradeoffs that impact the end result. One company submitted the requirements from its survey as follows:

- We want to conduct a survey for all employees.
- We want the survey to be short; but it needs to evaluate our values, the commitment of employees, satisfaction with their immediate supervisors, and other relevant issues.
- We don't want the survey to raise employee expectations.
- We don't want the review of survey results to slow this place down, so the reports should be issued at the division level (300 to 500 people).
- We want to see significant changes and improvements in the company's performance as a result of the survey from one year to the next.

Previous surveys had been conducted in the past using the same approach. The assessment of the prior surveys showed that: (1) The company generally saw no improvement in the survey results from year to year; (2) employee expectations for change were typically high, but when they saw little happening as a result of the surveys, morale began to fall; (3) executives found it difficult to track down specific data or to understand survey issues; and (4) top management often asked, "Why don't we see any improvement?"

The survey content and method of administration, the feedback process, and the actions taken or not taken afterward all have a significant impact on the outcome of a survey. Even modest changes in any of these processes can significantly impact the outcomes of a survey, and it is essential that managers clearly understand this before they plan to conduct a survey.

In this particular example, the company administered its survey to every employee. Having every employee complete a survey created a feeling of involvement and communicated employee perceptions to management. The process of asking all employees to participate also increased employee expectations. Many of the survey items which centered on company values caused the employees to consider the issues that occurred in their work groups. Items that asked if employees were treated with dignity and respect, or that asked if people were involved in decisions that affected them, were responded to positively by some groups and negatively by others. The employees responded to the questions enthusiastically. The process of responding created expectations about recognizing achievements and dealing with problems more effectively—the main issues raised by the survey.

However, in the company's efforts to make the feedback process efficient, it was decided to report the feedback in large group meetings of 300 to 500 people. Rather than identifying and focusing on work group issues, the average effect of the large group reports failed to identify the particular issues of any one work group. This frustrated many employees, who felt the company was ignoring the most important issues. The managers failed to see how the negative issues identified by the survey could have anything to do with bottom-line performance. Action plans were developed, but little effort or commitment was made to create meaningful change. None of the survey measures were inappropriate, but as a whole group, they were ineffective.

The content of a survey impacts how the results should be reported. The way a survey is administered affects the kinds of information that will be generated, the levels at which it should be reported back to the company, and the expectations employees will have about change. Aligning these processes makes the survey effort successful, while misalignment can cause more harm than good.

Before moving ahead with your survey, and to better understand the tradeoffs inherent in designing and conducting surveys, consider the four dimensions in Figure 4.1.

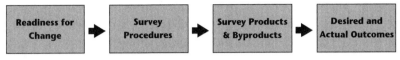

Figure 4.1: The four dimensions of surveys.

Healthy organizations with high employee trust and commitment will notice more impact in conducting a survey than organizations that are not healthy and well-managed. In extremely unhealthy organizations, where it may be very difficult to optimize survey procedures, employee surveys will often do more harm than good. To prepare your company for change, you should first consider these factors (for additional material, see Appendix: The Readiness for Change Profile):

Readiness for Change

In order for an organization to entertain using an employee survey process, there needs to be a minimal level of readiness. In organizations without a minimal level of readiness, the employee survey can do more harm than good. In organizations with a high level of readiness there are possibilities for substantially more change at an increased pace. The key elements of readiness are as follows:

Willingness for individuals to take initiative. An employee survey asks each employee who completes a survey to take the initiative to respond to the survey, provide valid evaluations and suggestions for change and improvement. In organizations where employees do not feel empowered or encouraged to take the initiative, the survey process becomes passive rather than active. Employees see the process as something that is being done to them rather than something in which they are active participants. The initiative becomes increasingly important in the action planning and change process.

High level of energy. In organizations that are "burned out," the survey just adds "insult to injury." A successful survey effort requires effort, energy, and commitment by those involved. The commitment of energy should be delivered with 20 percent focused on getting the survey completed and returned and 80 percent on analyzing results and taking action. After reviewing a proposal to design, administer, analyze, give feedback, and create change plans for a survey, a group of managers who were responsible for the project said the following, "This looks like a lot of work and a real commitment." Our response was, "You're absolutely correct." They then responded, "We just don't have the energy." The reality of energy in organizations is that it has little to do with the amount of work people have to do or the number of commitments they have to manage. People in organizations with the most work on their plate often have the most energy.

Organizational efficiency. In some organizations there is so much red tape, paperwork and bureaucracy that it is almost impossible to get anything done. Other organizations are stifled by a need for consensus on every issue. In highly inefficient organizations, the employee survey can be viewed as just more paperwork in an endless stream of requests or reports that don't seem to lead to any change. In organizations challenged by inefficiency, creating a survey process that is quick, simple, and easy can be a key to making the project successful.

A high level of employee commitment. Committed employees see an employee survey as a tool to help them achieve their goals and voice their concerns. Employees with low levels of commitment will see the survey as an inconvenience and a waste of money. A group of employees with a low level of commitment had the following suggestion, "Why not take all the money we spend on this survey and increase our salaries?" Their focus was,

"What's in this for me?" Unfortunately, the company couldn't increase any employee's pay until it figured out how to be more successful.

Informed and involved employees. Everyone likes to feel they are insiders. Insiders feel they are an important part of the company's success. They feel that their contribution is important. They feel others want their opinion. Outsiders feel tangential and an optional part of a process. They feel they are left behind, that others don't ask for their opinion, and that they are the last to know. Often on this dimension of readiness, an employee survey can provide a great benefit. Companies that have a highly involved and informed workforce use their employee survey as a tool to both communicate information and to involve employees in evaluating effectiveness.

Trust. Trust is critical for employee surveys to work well. A union group in a plant asked, "Why should we participate? We think that you will just use the data to vote out the union." A transportation company participated in a survey after having gone through a significant downsizing. Each survey had a tracking number on the form. Employees speculated that the tracking number would be able to identify them personally even though management denied that any tracking would be done. Employees speculated that the results would be used to do additional downsizing. Half of the employees completed surveys. A third of the surveys that were returned had their tracking numbers torn off. Another word for trust is faith. The survey process works only if a majority of people from top executives to employees believe that it can work. If people lack trust or the faith that issues will be seriously reviewed and honest efforts will be made to change, then the process will not be successful.

Optimism. Organizational optimism is created when there is a consistent record of success. Organizational pessimism is created when a company is finding it difficult to succeed. The feeling of optimism or pessimism can frequently determine an organization's ability to survive. While a certain level of paranoia is sometimes helpful and some pessimism can motivate people to take action, the persistence of organizational pessimism can often encourage people to leave the organization, either physically or emotionally.

Supportive relationships. Great things can be accomplished because of the commitment that is generated for strong personal relationships. Feeling supported and accepted is the foundation for trust, commitment, and the feeling of involvement. When people experience too many negative personal relationships, other aspects of readiness will most certainly lag behind.

The assessment of readiness for change can be done intuitively for an organization, but it can also be evaluated with the assistance of an instrument. The appendix contains the Readiness for Change Profile. This profile can be used to evaluate an organization's level of readiness.

Survey Procedures

Survey procedures involve a variety of processes and approaches. Each procedure can have an impact on both the products and byproducts of the survey, and on outcomes of the survey. The following survey procedures will impact the outcome of your survey:

Establish expectations up front. Surveys are never neutral. The very act of conducting an employee survey will cause employees to expect something to happen.[2] Each question builds this expectation to some degree. Results that are never acted upon or addressed violate those expectations. Therefore, only those issues that need to be changed should be included in a survey. Any survey efforts to address issues that will have only a marginal impact on an organization's ability to compete will divert energy and attention from more important issues.

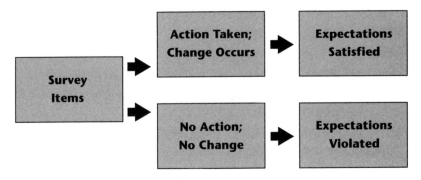

Figure 4.2: Survey items and expectations.

Even without all the additional questions that may divert energy and resources from the main issues in your survey, it will likely be impossible for you to change everything addressed by the survey. But, if your employees understand that the survey will be measuring many issues and that only a few will be resolved, then their expectations will be more realistic. Survey expectations will be satisfied if employees observe a significant change on a global organizational issue, or if they perceive a change on any issue that affects them personally, as a result of the survey. Also, if they observe a significant change on one issue, their expectations will be reduced in relation to other issues.

Deciding who will take surveys. A common debate is whether a survey should be distributed to all employees or only to a selected or random sample. The more employees complete surveys, the greater the expectations will be. Figure 4.3 shows the relationship between which employees were asked to complete a survey and how the results were shared throughout the organization.

	Broad Organization	Work Groups
Sample	Good Fit	Insufficient data to create group feedback reports
All Employees	Expectations raised but issues only reviewed in large groups	Good Fit

Figure 4.3: How results are shared with employees.

The figure shows a "Good Fit" for conducting the survey using a random sample of all employees, provided the results are reviewed at broad organizational levels. By asking only a limited number of employees to respond to the surveys, the expectation level is minimized. In this case, a random sample is preferred, because when companies ask all their employees to participate but then summarize the results at the organizational level, they face a strong possibility that employee expectations will be violated.

Picture yourself completing a survey, answering items that reflect a source of frustration for yourself and your work group. If the results of that survey are reviewed and analyzed only at the division level, your particular work group is compiled into a sweeping generalization that includes all the other work groups in the division. The unique issues in your work group have little chance of surfacing at the division level. Only issues that are consistent from one group to another would surface at high levels of aggregation.

Figure 4.4 shows the distribution of results for a division with 67 work units. The average score for the division is 3.68, but work group results range from 2.75 to 4.38.

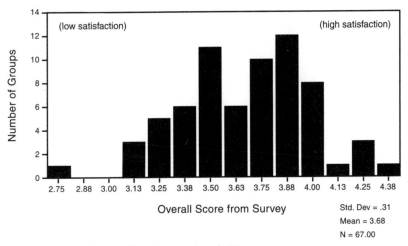

Figure 4.4: Distribution of work groups in a division.

Figure 4.4 is typical of many organizations. It is a vivid representation of the wide range of results that occur across an organization. Some groups are very negative, and others are very positive. Aggregating the results at the organization or large-division level depicts only the average of all the data compiled. It loses the detail of the individual work groups and the other demographic factors. The advantage of reviewing results in large groups is that it simplifies the feedback process. The disadvantage is that aggregation of data may hide significant variations in work group results.

Figure 4.5 demonstrates what can happen when aggregating survey results.

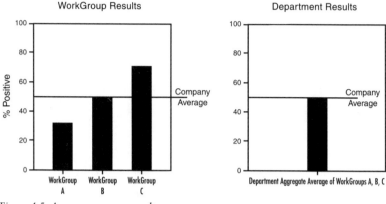

Figure 4.5: Aggregare survey results.

The work group results on the left show data for three work groups. Note how group A is much more negative than the company average, while group C is much more positive. If the results are analyzed only at the company or department level, these differences disappear, as is shown in the figure on the right. Employees for group A are likely to feel that their issues are being ignored, and group C is likely to wonder why the results were not more positive. Group B will believe nothing is wrong at all. If results are not examined at the work group level, action plans for groups A and C cannot be properly developed.

Sharing results with employees. Aggregating survey results into broad organizational units provides an efficient means of processing feedback. But, as Figure 4.4 demonstrates, it also hides smaller work group issues. Feedback at the organizational level will leave many work group issues unresolved and unexamined, leading to employee expectations being violated. On the other hand, supplying feedback to every work group in an organization can be a large undertaking.

One manager described her company feedback process to each work group as, "We shut down the company to feed back the survey results and generate action plans."

Other companies have created more efficient processes to supply feedback to work groups. When results are given to the work groups, the issues for the group are clearly displayed but require the manager and group members to work through the issues on their own time.

Another consideration, when deciding at which level results are to be shared, relates to the content of the survey. Survey items may have a broad or a narrow focus. For example, the following items tend to have a broad focus:

- I understand where this organization is going in the future.
- The way work is assigned frequently leads to poor collaboration between work groups.
- All things considered, the organization's benefits package (insurance, retirement, vacation time, and so forth), excluding pay, is fair.
- This organization is willing to experiment with new approaches.

Other items have a work group focus:

- I get sufficient information about what is going on in other departments and functions to do my job effectively.
- My work group seems to have the right mix of talented people to get the job done right.
- I receive appropriate training for the work I do.
- My immediate manager balances concern for productivity and results with a concern for my needs.

Items with a narrow focus address specific work group issues. When employees respond to items such as these, the items tend to generate expectations for change in the work group. Therefore, when results are compiled at levels higher than the work group level, people in the work groups do not see any attention given to their specific results. If strengths and weaknesses are consistent across work groups, then aggregate reports can reflect work group concerns. But in general, it is very unusual that work group results are consistent throughout the organization. In fact, most companies note a high level of variability.

Also, when the results of employee surveys are aggregated, it is impossible for work groups to know whether or not the results of their group were unique. Consequently, many work groups play a guessing game as they review the aggregate reports, wondering if the results accurately reflect their issues—or even if the information is relevant to them at all.

Figure 4.6 shows the relationship between the focus of a survey and the way survey results are shared with employees.

	Broad Organization	**Down to Work Groups**
Strategic/Global Organizational Issues	**Good Fit**	**Survey results are difficult to act on at a work group level**
Work Group Issues	**Variation between work groups causes expectations violation**	**Good Fit**

Figure 4.6: *How the survey focus affects sharing of results.*

When survey results are shared at the organizational level, it is best to keep the items generally focused on strategic and global organization issues. And when survey results are shared with employees at the work group level, it is best to focus on work group issues. Most off-the-shelf surveys contain both types of items. When the content of survey items matches the level at which results are shared, then the survey has a better chance of satisfying the expectations raised by the survey.

Responsibility for taking action. The level at which results are shared with employees tends to dictate who is responsible for taking action. If a survey is conducted and the results are shared only with top management, then recommendations for action need to come from top management. Effective top-level executives can involve the entire organization in change efforts, but they keep the responsibility for initiating the change. The more levels that share data in an organization, the greater the opportunity to push responsibility for initiating change down through the organization.[3] If change is the desired outcome of a survey and the change requires the cooperation of all employees, then two principles must be kept in mind:

- The greater the number of people involved in the change effort, the higher the probability of change.
- Changes that occur closest to employees are the ones that will be noted and remembered.

I am often amused by politicians who talk about great changes that have occurred: Crime is down, roads are improved, the city is providing better service. When I hear this speech, my criteria for believing it comes from my personal circumstances. Is crime really down in my neighborhood? Have the roads that lead to my street been improved? Have I experienced better service from the city? The more distant the changes, and the fewer personal experiences I have with the described changes, the less I believe that changes have occurred.

Likewise, in work situations, employees are most affected by the changes that occur in their work group. When employees have a negative situation in their work group that remains unchanged, they have a difficult time agreeing that positive changes have occurred elsewhere in the organization. Top management may talk about significant changes at the top of the organization, but if the immediate situation remains unchanged at the work group level, the employees will not see eye to eye with management.

Using surveys to measure trends or begin change initiatives. While most employee surveys talk about measuring issues that will result in change, some organizations approach the assessment process as more of a trend-tracking process than a strong initiative for change. I was recently approached by a company to develop a 15-item survey that would be given to a small random sample of employees every quarter. This company referred to the survey as a "pulse." When the company proposed the project, they envisioned senior management receiving results every quarter and making appropriate changes. My advice on the project was to present the survey concept to both management and employees as a means of tracking historical trends rather than as an initiative for change.

With a small random sample on a few items, it becomes extremely difficult to respond to small variations in survey results from quarter to quarter. Over longer intervals, however, trends make more sense.

The main problem with pulse-type surveys is managing the expectations for change. The more frequently surveys are administered, the higher the expectations. With a very small sample and only a few survey items, managers tend to react more to the events that occurred in the quarter than the actual survey items. For example, if results drop significantly from one quarter to another, managers may attribute the data to a large reorganization.

Most managers prefer this simple cause-and-effect model because it is easy to interpret: Specific changes in the organization affected employees either positively or negatively in the quarter. But although the cause-and-effect approach occasionally works, it is actually quite difficult to determine scientifically valid cause-and-effect relationships.

Typically, many events will have occurred during the quarter that would have had some impact on employee satisfaction. Some are internal initiatives, others come from competitors, and still others come from the external environment (the economy, markets and exchanges, consumer trends, and so forth). This makes responding to a quarterly "pulse" survey very difficult. However, if the process is kept low profile, it can produce an interesting measure to track over time.

Another way to conduct a pulse survey is to design survey items to focus on some work group issues as well as a few broad company issues. To do this, take a random sample of the work groups in the company, but provide surveys to all of the members of each group selected to take the survey. The results of the survey would be reported to each work group, and the work groups would be responsible to develop action plans for the issues uncovered. The aggregate of all work group results are then delivered to top management for tracking purposes.

This approach satisfies the expectations raised by the survey by causing changes to occur in work groups, and it also allows for aggregate data to be presented to top management. Top management can then use the aggregate data for tracking purposes with much less pressure to show the meaningful changes resulting from a quarterly survey. Eventually, all work groups would have the opportunity to participate in the survey.

Frequency of surveys. Several years ago I visited with a former classmate from graduate school. He described the relationship he has with his boss and how he manages it:

> About once a week my boss calls down and asks
> me to come to his office. I drop everything, grab

a notepad, and run upstairs. He usually
describes at least 10 things I ought to be working on, and I capture each one in great detail. I
make sure I am clear about each of the direc-
tives and what should be done. Then I go back
to my office and file the list. I don't work on
any of the initiatives because I have too many
other things to do.

After a few weeks, my boss calls again and usually asks about one of the initiatives. I tell him
that I am concluding some initial work and will
have something on his desk in a few days. I then
drop everything and work on that one initiative
until I finish. He never brings up the other nine,
and I never do anything about them.

I believe my friend's experience with his boss is similar
to many other manager-employee relationships. It depicts
what happens to the variety of initiatives and efforts put
forth by managers in organizations, and how their
employees typically handle those initiatives.

Conducting employee surveys without any indication
that the process will occur again sends the message that
the survey is a "one-time" process, merely the "flavor-of-
the-month" initiative. The effectiveness of a survey is frequently affected when both managers and employees sit
back and wait to see if the survey just goes away like so
many other programs over the years.

Before conducting a survey, one of the first questions
organizations should ask is, "Will we ever conduct the survey again?" If the answer is yes, then that information
should be communicated to employees at the time they take
the survey. Simply knowing that the survey will be used
again, and that they are not just the latest change initiative,

will help the employees feel some consistency. It also sends a very positive message to managers: If management receives negative results and makes no effort to change, they will get caught, because the second survey will still show the results to be negative, and maybe even more negative.

My friend has never been caught by his boss. His boss apparently never remembered the nine other things that needed to be done. He was busy enough with other things that he did not want to bother with the nine other items. Most managers in organizations have learned the same lessons as my friend. They learned that, to survive, you must pace yourself and figure out where you might to get caught.

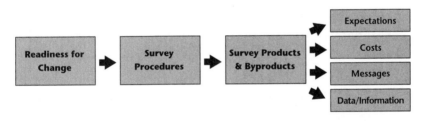

Figure 4.7: Survey products and byproducts.

Survey Products and Byproducts

An organization's readiness for change and its survey procedures affect the survey's main products: communications and information.

A survey has the ability to communicate information throughout the organization. Each item has the potential to send an important message: "This survey is important. What is your opinion about how the company performs?" The process of responding to survey items creates an effective learning process for employees, because information is presented, responded to, measured, analyzed, and then reported to employees in the feedback process. The information is valuable to the extent that it is understandable, concise, unbiased, and linked to the issues that drive business performance.

In addition, two byproducts also result from surveys: employee expectations and costs.

Expectations. Expectations are not necessarily negative byproducts of a survey. They can motivate employees and managers and encourage change. But if high expectations are violated, the result is anger, disappointment, frustration, and cynicism. No one wants to waste their time on activities that will be ignored.

Costs. The costs are not only those associated with processing surveys, but also the unmeasured costs associated with completing surveys, reacting to feedback, and making changes.

Ultimately, any proposed activity comes down to the question, "Can the benefits and outcomes justify the costs?" Often, surveys generate activities and actions that create great benefits for the organization, but people tend to forget the starting point was the employee survey. The more companies will do to link desired outcomes with the survey process, the clearer it will be to leaders why survey efforts should continue.

Messages. Employee surveys offer companies a unique opportunity to send a positive message to the employees who complete the surveys. The most frequent message organizations try to convey is, "This company values employee opinions." But sometimes the message sent is unintended. For example, one employee made the following remark regarding a survey experience: "The survey was sent to a select group of employees. I did not get one. The person in the cubicle next to me got one, which made me wonder why management was not interested in my opinion. This really made me mad."

Surveys may also be used to reinforce several different messages. A large manufacturer conducting an employee survey wanted to reinforce the message that quality was the most important objective in the plant. To help reinforce that message, the following item was constructed:

> This next section presents pairs of statements. Please indicate which of the two statements you believe is a higher priority to your immediate manager by marking the corresponding number: (1 or 2). Even though you may perceive that both statements are equally emphasized, you need to select one. In such cases, it may be useful to ask, "If a situation arose where only one of the two statements could be satisfied, which of the two would be satisfied?"

79. COST (reducing the total price of our products and services) or SCHEDULE (producing our products and services on time, meeting a deadline)

80. SCHEDULE (producing our products and services on time, meeting a deadline) or QUALITY (meeting design specifications and customer expectations)

81. QUALITY (meeting design specifications and customer expectations) or COST (reducing the total price of our products and services)

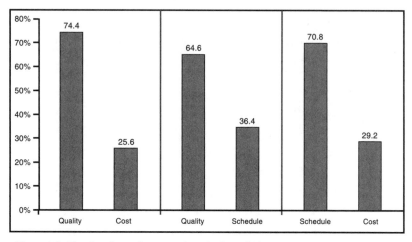

Figure 4.8: The data from the survey item is charted above.

The process of presenting a pointed question and reviewing the results helped this organization reinforce the message of quality over cost and schedule. Although the majority of employees made the appropriate tradeoff, not everyone did. This generated discussions about whether pressures to lower costs and meet schedules were forcing employees to make the wrong decisions.

Other messages communicated by surveys may reinforce values, clarify strategies, and emphasize safety.[4] I like the way movie producers can convey the entire message of a 90-minute film in a single sentence. For example, "Boy meets girl and falls in love." I think organizations should learn to do the same thing prior to conducting surveys. Examples include:

- We want all employees to give their best thinking on how we are performing on a few key issues.
- Tell top management how they can run this company better.
- Each group: Evaluate your effectiveness.
- Let's reinforce the importance of living our values.

These are a few samples of the messages managers usually intend to communicate in conducting a survey. Keep in mind that the content of the survey, and the survey procedures used, also send messages. These unwritten messages, often unintended, are also communicated. And, if you are not careful, they may conflict with and override the message you intend to send.

For example, an organization wanted all of its many employees to complete a survey. Management decided the best way to get everyone to take the survey would be to require all employees to attend a meeting in the conference room to complete the survey. A roll was taken at the start of the meeting before the surveys were passed out. Each employee was required to complete the survey and return it to the survey administrator. The unintended message sent to the employees was, "We do not trust you."

The organization's culture, however, provided employees with a high level of flexibility and freedom. Very few things had ever been mandated. The person in charge of the survey had been acting on advice from another organization that had successfully administered surveys the same way. But, in this company, the process not only sent an unintended message, it negatively impacted the data.

In another example, a software company was in a great hurry to administer a survey. Inadvertently, managers conducting the survey had overlooked enclosing any communication with the survey prior to sending it in the company mail. As employees opened the survey, they only saw a simple note from the president. So, because no one in the company had heard anything about the survey, most employees felt that the survey was not very important. The message sent was: "You don't have to fill it out if you have better things to do." The return rate for the survey was less than 50 percent.

Data/Information. Fundamentally, the main reason organizations conduct surveys is to collect information. Surveys can be very helpful in getting an accurate picture of organizational strengths and weaknesses. Some people question the usefulness of employee surveys. They note that good managers and executives can keep in touch with employees and know their opinions by simply talking with employees regularly. And, while having managers and executives keep in touch with employees is always desirable, even well-informed managers can benefit from survey data.

Surveys provide structure to the collection of employee opinions. The ability of a survey to measure differences between groups and evaluate strengths and weaknesses between one item and another makes it a valuable tool in assisting managers to do an effective job. Surveys also capture the opinions of all participants at the same point in time and on the same issues. Most informal discussions with employees do not have that same rigor.

What Information Do You Want?

Information that is understandable. It is very frustrating when you go through all the difficulties of collecting survey information to review the results and find it is not clear what a positive or negative result means. The following item was the second most negative item in a survey: "I can find the time I need to further develop my skills and abilities."

When the data was reviewed, no one was sure whether the negative response to this item had anything to do with organizational practices or whether it recognized the fact that most people don't have a lot of spare time. The organization concluded that if they were to arrange work for people where they could answer this item positively, they would most likely be underutilized.

Concise information. Each item in a survey represents a cost: the time to complete each item, the time to analyze the results, the time to review the feedback by each group, and the time to prepare action items. Finding a process to ask the right questions in the right quantity makes the survey process more useful and acceptable for all employees in the organization. After reviewing many surveys, it appears that the survey is designed like a large fishing net. The logic seems to be, "If we ask enough items, we will find something significant." This process is very expensive and also an enormous distraction.

Another common practice in employee surveys is to use multiple response scales: First, asking a survey item and then assessing whether the issue is important; second, asking if the issue needs to be changed or improved. We have frequently found that while the multiple scales do provide some additional information, the additional insight is not substantial.

Assessing one two-scaled instrument we found that the inclusion of the two scales only added 3 percent additional information. Of the insight gained by the survey, 97 percent could be gathered from one scale. The inclusion of two scales increased the response time of employees and complicated the analysis of results, but for very little additional insight.

Information linked to strategic direction. Information collected from an employee survey and linked to the strategy of the company can provide an effective forecast of issues that may get in the way of strategic success. Information that is not closely linked to the future of the company tends not to receive as much attention.

Information appropriate to the purpose of the survey. The most effective surveys are those with a point of view and purpose. The worst surveys are those that have five different purposes and multiple sponsors. Surveys can accomplish multiple purposes, but one group needs to make decisions for the overall survey product. Too often, surveys with multiple sponsors hold each other hostage and feel that they deserve an equal number of items and attention.

What Information Do You Want to Avoid?

Information that is biased. Interviews with employees about previous survey efforts have revealed comments such as, "They designed the survey to tell them what they wanted to hear." "They avoided asking the real questions or addressing the real problems facing this organization." "I thought this was a pretty good place to work, but the survey results were so negative I could not believe the data was correct." A survey needs the appropriate balance of positive and negative issues. A survey without any positives leaves the impression of failure. A survey with no weaknesses provides nothing to improve.

Too much or too little information. Every survey needs to fit the audience. I once worked with a researcher in graduate school, and we designed a survey with over 500 items. We were on a major "fishing expedition." The survey was administered in a research lab, and the researchers did not seem to mind the length. I have administered 50-item surveys in other settings and had people complain about the length. Shorter is not always better. In designing surveys, I often meet with committees who are determined to shorten their surveys regardless of the quality of the data they will get back. Once the surveys are completed, this editing process often leaves their companies asking for additional clarification on what the real issues are.

Information from unknown sources. There can be a big difference between a small random sample, and a low survey-return rate. In a survey with a small random sample, you select who will complete the survey. In a survey with a low return rate, the employees decide who completes the survey. The process of choosing to complete a survey or not is not always random, using the statistical definition of the term. It is much more difficult to reach accurate conclusions from surveys with a low return rate because you are never sure if the data represents the organization as a whole or just the specific group of individuals that completed the surveys.

Information that is misleading. People will not generally make negative comments about themselves. The following item was the most positive item in a survey. "I am prepared to be accountable for the decisions of my work." This led the organization to believe people felt accountable. But, upon observing behavior in the organization, senior management was led to another conclusion. A careful reading of the item shows that the question did not ask if people were accountable for their decisions, but only if they were "prepared to be accountable." Who would respond negatively to this item?

Another item indicated very positive results: "I understand what decisions I can make myself and those which require approval from others." But, do these positive results come because everyone clearly understands which decisions they can make, or are they only responding positively because responding negatively would make them look stupid?

Survey data can be very valuable. It can inspire change, direct efforts, point out problems, reveal strengths, confirm issues, communicate directions, and challenge employees to find new ways of thinking. But, if they are not designed or conducted correctly, surveys can also raise expectations that never get resolved, that reinforce strategies of the past, that are complex or hard to understand, or that are burdensome to managers.

Desired and Actual Outcomes

I was once invited to talk with the president of a large company to discuss conducting an employee survey. (I'll refer to him as president #1.) My first question was, "Why do you want to conduct a survey?"

He responded, "This is a large organization, and I frankly don't have a clue what is going on out there in terms of what employees think."

"It sounds like you want an assessment that measures employee opinions," I said.

"That's right."

I asked, "What if we find something you don't like?"

"Well, then I'll change that," he replied.

In a separate company, I interviewed the president of a company that was preparing to develop a new employee survey. (I'll refer to him as president #2.) I asked him, "What do you want to get out of this survey project?"

He replied, "We are in the process of implementing a new strategy. In order to implement this strategy we need several critical organizational capabilities. I want to evaluate from our employees' perspective our effectiveness in these capabilities. The survey should focus the attention of the entire company on these issues and what we can do to improve them."

President #1 is on a fishing expedition. On this expedition the company will use a large net, and whatever it catches will be discussed. Eventually the managers will have to decide what to do with what they catch: keep and use whatever it is, or throw it back. The desired outcome for that survey is information. I cannot guarantee the information they find will help the organization be more productive or effective, but I can guarantee that the employees will have some expectations for change on issues that are measured.

President #2 is also on a fishing expedition. The difference is that this president is fishing for a specific variety of fish with a particular bait using a fly rod. The desired outcome of his survey is to improve a few specific organizational capabilities. The clearer the objective of the survey and the desired outcomes, the more likely the companies are to achieve those outcomes.

Listed below are a few commonly desired outcomes and the challenges associated with achieving each. The keys to achieving each outcome are also listed.

Information/Trends Tracking:

Challenge: How do we gather information without raising expectations?

Keys: Use a very light random sampling. Keep a low profile for the survey; maintain clarity about what will be done with results; help top management understand its role in reviewing the results, recommending changes, and communicating with employees about the survey.

Change:

Challenge: How can we keeping the survey focused on the right issues?

Keys: Target the survey to those issues. Drive data down the organization; find root causes at the organization level; teach managers to deal with, prioritize, and share feedback, and to implement action plans.

Improved Employee Morale:

Challenge: What do we do when "grumbles" seem to be the key issues, and few managers stick with change efforts because those efforts don't help them solve day-to-day problems?

Keys: Avoid the "bottomless pits": stress, balance, amount of pay. Focus on issues linked to the company's strategy, improving productivity or efficiency; select the issues you can do something about.

Benchmarking:

Challenge: How do we assess items in benchmark comparisons to see if they are linked to strategy?

Keys: Find benchmark items that fit your company's core issues. Make sure this does not become an academic exercise of, "How do we compare?" The real issue of the survey should be, "Where does this organization need to be, and what issues need to change?" Make sure people keep in perspective what forms the benchmarks and what conclusions can be drawn. Too often, when survey items are benchmarked, top management concludes that results are equivalent and, therefore, no action is necessary. Thus, the company never achieves a competitive advantage.

Evaluate Program Effectiveness *(benefits, communications procedures, rewards, etc.):*

Challenge: How do we handle "extra information" that managers want in the survey?

Keys: Keep it short and simple. Design the questions in a way that won't detract from the rest of the survey. Then manage expectations; don't allow the group requesting the addition to take complete control over the content.

Assessing Survey Outcomes

Desired outcomes are not always achieved. Generally speaking, if you could measure the actual outcomes from most employee surveys, there would be little justification for continuing the practice. When employee surveys create more negative side effects than positive outcomes, the surveys can hardly be justified. The process of assessing actual outcomes can be accomplished through focus groups that evaluate the actual versus desired outcomes from the survey. The focus groups begin prior to the survey's administration, and then reevaluate immediately after the survey's administration, after the feedback process, and finally a few months after the survey process is over.

Focus groups tend to be influenced by one or two vocal or influential members. I have participated in several focus groups that were generally positive and concluded things were going well. Then I conducted another focus group where one group member was very vocal, and the group turned mostly negative. Be sure to conduct enough focus groups to get a fair opinion. The questions for each focus group session should include:

Prior to Survey Administration:

1. Do employees know a survey is being conducted?

2. What is the "word on the street" about why the survey is being conducted?

3. Have the employees seen any official message about the survey?

4. How much confidence do the employees have about the official message?

After Completing the Survey:

1. What are the employees' general reactions to the survey?

2. In the opinion of employees, what messages did the survey convey?

3. Did employees receive different messages than the ones intended?

4. What do employees believe will happen because of this survey?

5. Are the employees optimistic or pessimistic that something will happen?

After Initial Feedback:

1. Do employees feel the feedback is open, honest, and straightforward?

2. Do employees agree the issues selected for change are high priority issues?

3. Do employees have confidence that something will change?

4. Do employees feel they personally have a role in helping to make changes?

Three Months Later:

1. Do employees draw any links between the survey and a change or improvement effort?

2. Are employees aware of any actions that are being worked on?

3. Has the employee survey affected them personally?

Summary

Newton's Third Law of Motion states: For every force on an object, there will always be an equal and opposite force exerted by that object.

The purpose of this chapter was to uncover the complex actions and reactions created by employee surveys. Understanding the consequences of various actions (such as survey items included, who was asked, how results were shared, how action was taken, and so forth) and the reactions of employees to those actions will help ensure that desired outcomes are achieved.

Notes to Chapter Four

1. Nanci Hellmich, "Time Stackers." *USA Today*. May 28, 1997, 1D.

2. David A. Nadler, *Feedback and Organization Development: Using Data-Based Methods*. Reading, MA: Addison-Wesley, 1977, 65.

3. Ibid, 154-65.

4. Allen I. Kraut and Allen J. Kraut, *Organizational Surveys: Tools for Assessment and Change*. San Francisco: Jossey-Bass, 1996, 10.

CHAPTER FIVE

The Steering Committee: Key to Success

In strategic-alignment surveys, the steering committee is a key factor in accomplishing the objectives of the change process. Members of the committee represent, and provide access to, a variety of employee groups. A well-rounded steering committee will have representatives who provide leadership in their respective groups, which drives the survey process from a special interest group-sponsored event to a companywide event.

Steering committees are composed of 8 to 10 people in the company who represent various demographic groups (or locations). The composition of the committee is critical for its success. Members of the committee must accept the responsibility, and have the authority, to make changes necessary for a high-performance organization. Selecting committee representatives from major groups in a company improves the effectiveness of the committee. The committee members need to be well-respected idea leaders in their groups, with either formal or informal power.

Some committees are composed of management only, while others include hourly or union representatives on the committee. The most effective committees have similar characteristics to the demographic makeup of the company. An effective steering committee provides leadership, efficiency, clarity, guidance, analysis, and perspective to the company.

Two Cases

The impact of a steering committee's members, and the corresponding impact of the support the committee receives, are demonstrated in the following two cases:

Company A. At the beginning of a survey project, a steering committee was commissioned. Members were selected from each division, but none from high levels in the organization. Senior managers and executives were apparently "too busy" to be part of the committee.

Committee members were bright, enthusiastic, and willing to do whatever it would take to make the project a success. Interviews were conducted, and key issues were identified by the steering committee in preparation for survey design. Based on the key issues, a customized survey was developed. The steering committee worked hard to develop a survey that would fit the needs of the whole organization, and to finish the work within the agreed-upon deadlines.

After the survey was completed, managers from throughout the organization began to express their concerns and wanted an opportunity to review the survey. The review process added an additional month to the survey development time. It also allowed each of the managers to add their particular issues of interest to the survey, which made the survey less focused and strategic. After the senior managers had finished the reviews, a vice president in charge of the project decided he didn't like the length of the survey and singlehandedly cut 20 survey items.

The steering committee began to feel totally disenfranchised from the project. Although they realized that their decision needed approval, decisions had been made on the project without even asking for their input. And though the team members were bright and capable, they began to feel very negative. They felt that they had been asked to guide the project, but their opinions were not valued.

Company B. A steering committee was formed to guide the development, administration, and survey feedback of an employee survey. Members of the committee included two high-level managers, as well as several middle managers and line employees. One member of the committee, a production manager, was known to be critical about the survey process.

The first committee meeting was designed to inform group members of their roles and expectations, which were high. Members were expected to attend each meeting and adjust their schedules around the steering committee's needs. Each of the members agreed to the roles and expectations and made the necessary commitments. At the meeting members also discussed the goals of the survey, and the committee developed a vision for how the survey could become a critical force in improving the organization. Committee members also discussed, from the employees' perspective, what would benefit the average employee.

The committee members saw their roles as influence leaders throughout the company, and the committee felt strongly that this survey would be their survey. Interviews were conducted, and results were reviewed carefully. Key drivers of organizational success were agreed upon by the committee and then shared with the executive management team. Survey items were developed and then tested, and once again the survey was review by the executive management team with a few minor changes.

The survey was developed and administered quickly and achieved a high level of focus. Employees at all levels of the organization felt that the survey had been an excellent tool to foster change. The project time line was met each step of the way. The survey was perceived positively by each group in the company, and one year after its first administration the results from the second survey showed significant improvement in the company's critical measures.

Building a High-Performance Steering Committee

The effectiveness of steering committees varies widely between companies, as shown in these two cases. Some committees are highly effective, while others seem to drag projects down with them. Randy Stott, a managing director at Novations Group, Inc., has found (and I have confirmed in my own experience) that high-performance steering committees have the following characteristics and behaviors:

High-performance steering committees are linked directly to the main business of the company. Too often, unsuccessful survey projects are linked to functional areas or the specific needs of special-interest groups, and consequently they are viewed as "HR," "training," or "organizational effectiveness" programs. When steering committee members are drawn only from human resources, they tend to focus only on HR issues and the overall effectiveness of the committee is greatly diminished. The problem with these projects is that they don't have any line support. Those people directly linked to the main business don't see the survey as an essential piece of their business. Steering committees are more effective when they:

• *Focus on creating a competitive advantage for the business.* By communicating that the survey will help make employees happier, or because "it's the right thing to do," creates false assumptions about strategic-alignment surveys. Steering committees must communicate that the survey will help improve the business's competitive advantage.

• *Understand customer needs.* Steering committee members must understand that the purpose of a competitive advantage is to help the company build customer demand for its products or services.

• *Are willing to take risks and try different things.* Effective survey efforts must often apply unique approaches. Committee members must be willing to approach issues differently than in the past.

• *Are driven by challenges and the passion to improve.* Significant changes can occur when the steering committee wants itself—and the business—to be the best. When committees are motivated to perform only reasonably well, or to maintain the status quo, the opportunities for significant change are greatly diminished.

High-performance committees have a passion for progress. Surveys have a unique tendency to get bogged down in politics, administrative complexities, and other problems. At any given time, forces in the company or in various departments may be highly resistant to surveys being conducted. Committees place the success of a survey in jeopardy when they demand accuracy on every issue before moving ahead. Effective steering committees move their projects forward when they:

• *Recognize the value of speed in conducting surveys.* Ineffective committees don't have a sense for the value of employee time. They tend to accept delays or requests for additional time with little resistance. Highly effective committees are constantly racing the clock. They realize the value of their own time and the time of others in the company.

• *Gain approval to move ahead rapidly.* In one company that developed a customized survey, the process of agreeing on the final survey took about six months. The survey was constantly reviewed, revised, reviewed again, and sent to executives (who also reviewed and revised), and so forth. Such situations can kill an otherwise well-orchestrated project.

• *Design prototypes.* It is always difficult to know if something will work well before it is used. This is especially true when working conceptual programs such as surveys or feedback reports. Such programs are easier to test and improve through the use of prototypes, which may be reviewed, tested, and revised quickly.

• *Move forward in the face of ambiguity.* Lack of certainty has defeated many projects. Steering committees must be able to handle ambiguity and take action. Ambiguity occurs when someone says, "I don't think this is what the president wants," or "Will this really help?" or "Are we going to get anything out of this project?" In such environments, moving forward quickly often means the difference between making needed changes happen or allowing the status quo to dominate. Waiting to address every concern will often create unwanted delays and defeat innovative efforts to improve the company.

High-performance committees have high-impact leadership. Although having a strong leader may be helpful, leadership in a steering committee should not be centered on one person. Roles must be shared within the team.

An oil refinery with a long history of union-management conflict decided to conduct an employee survey. At the start of the project the survey was reviewed by the union. The union committee's recommendation was that the union would not fight against the survey, and management viewed this move as a strong vote of confidence.

As the steering committe was formed, one member recommended adding two union representatives to the committee. Others on the committee voiced considerable concern because they felt the union would do more to delay and disrupt the process than help. But the objections were overruled, and two union members were selected to represent the union on the committee.

The two union representatives had reputations for being negative and adversarial. As the committee began its work, the two union representatives were quiet but, when asked for their opinions, spoke freely. To the surprise of the union members, other members of the committee listened to them and asked helpful questions. The committee had a strong desire to make this survey a project that would really make a difference. The committee was convinced that to do this, they would need the involvement of all employees.

The union committee members found that their opinions were dealt with in an open and honest manner. Not all of their suggestions were implemented, but many were included in the final survey. As members of the committee, they frequently told other union members about their involvement on the committee, and, off the record, reported that the survey seemed to be a good and worthy project that would result in a better work environment. Their involvement provided significant leadership to union members.

High-impact leadership means that committees:

• *Drive the vision and set goals.* Steering committees must share a vision for what the survey will accomplish. Low-performance committees focus on the execution of steps, rather than on the bigger picture of significantly improving company effectiveness. For a team to have a larger vision it must first know the requirements for success and then define the project's goals. The committee must link the survey to the company's strategy and clearly define the freedom it has to design and implement the survey.

• *Build and sustain the team.* Steering committees are not one member; they are teams. Having the right players on the team is a critical aspect of a committee's success. The right groups must be represented, and those groups do not always include executives. Committee members must be able to influence the various constituencies: employee groups, unions, technical experts, company veterans, and so forth. After the members are selected, the team must set demanding standards for itself. These standards must be clear so that team members know what is expected. The work may be set up so the committee has to work as a team, or it may be modular so team members can work independently. In either case, the work needs to be synchronized. The committee will need adequate resources, in terms of people, budgets, and time, to execute the project effectively.

• *Champion the purpose of the survey.* All team members must believe in the cause for which the survey is designed. Too often, surveys get off to poor starts when committee members say they are "part of a stupid project that is going nowhere." Such negative comments often spread across the organization and doom survey efforts to failure. In addition to belief in the project, team members must be highly visible in the organization and have credibility in other parts of the company.

• *Enlist support rather than exercise control.* Survey projects require the support of many people in the organization. This support must never be demanded or mandated. High-performance committees are effective at eliciting support from various groups throughout the company, convincing them of the projects merits and potential results.

Characteristics of Team Members

One of my former class members went to work for a very large corporation. After he had worked as a change agent for several years, I asked him what it was like working for the large company. He responded, "It's like shooting a missile into a 5-million-pound marshmallow. The missile goes in and it explodes, but the marshmallow just wiggles and goes 'bloop.'" In large organizations, people often begin to feel that they have little impact. Unfortunately this belief causes many to just go through the motions of trying, dooming any worthy project to failure before it starts.

Causing an organization to change is difficult, but it's not impossible. Steering committees can have substantial influence on an organization, but only if its members have the desire to make a difference. Having the right team members is critical to steering committee success. But once team members have been selected, they must also understand their roles.

The steering committee sponsor. The committee sponsor may not actually be a team member. Usually the sponsor is an executive, often the CEO or department head, that gives the steering committee its authority and initial direction. The sponsor should:

• *Establish general goals, help select committee members, and then back off.* The only way the team can function as a team is for the sponsor to let them work.

• *Build support in the organization.* The sponsor must show support for his or her peers and others at all levels of the organization—and not just moral support, but resources, including financing and personnel. Building support also requires regular communication with the team.

• *Provide backup when needed.* Inevitably, someone in the company will resist the survey. When this happens, sponsors must provide active support. For example, resistance often occurs when someone selected for the steering committee is barred by a supervisor from participation because of the person's importance to that department, or because the time commitment would be too great. In such cases, the sponsor's action or inaction sends a strong message about the importance of the survey to the company. Persuasive action reinforces the importance of the survey, while inaction or ineffective action often sends the message "maybe this survey isn't very important."

• *Make sure the survey results in meaningful change.* Successful projects worth repeating are those that deliver significant and meaningful improvements to the company and establish a competitive advantage for the company.

The steering committee leader. The leader of the steering committee should:

- *Clearly understand the company's business strategy and direction.* The leader also should have business savvy not only in a particular department or function but in all functions and aspects of the enterprise.
- *Set high performance standards* for team members and other participants in the project.
- *Be able to make tough calls in the face of ambiguity.* The leader must be willing to remove team members who are not performing, and reject suggestions for new survey content (even if from an executive) that does not fit the direction of the survey effort.
- *Establish realistic goals and communicate them clearly* to committee members and project participants.
- *Keep the team focused on its mission.* Often, steering committees get caught up in solving problems unrelated to the survey project.

Committee members. The members of the steering committee should:

1. *Have strong reputations for being the best at what they do.*
- *Set high standards for themselves.*
- *Be willing to take risks and not stop in the face of unexpected problems.*
- *Push their points of view but be willing to accept the team's approach when decisions have been made.* Sometimes team members must be leaders, but other times they must be willing to support the leadership of others.
- *Commit themselves to, and believe in, the project.* Members must be able to see how, if surveys are conducted properly, they can add great value to the organization.
- *Have a passion for winning.*
- *Be the type of people who "aim to set world records, not just finish the race."*

Keys for Success

Experience has proven that, unless some key people in the company are willing to "sign up" to ensure that the changes are managed, coordinated, and paid adequate attention, the whole process has a slim chance of success.

Again, the membership of the steering committee depends upon the level of change desired. For example, if a company wishes to pursue strategic alignment for the total company, a very senior group may be desired. Decisions about the mission, business strategy, and actions of key managers will require the involvement of those with the required information and clout. The steering committee must:

• *Balance perspective* with knowledge and information from employees.

• *Spend time with people* at all levels in the company, building perspective about where the company is going.

• *Link the survey process* to the business and mission of the company.

• *Manage the overall strategic change process* in a manner which is congruent with the overall mission.

• *Keep the process focused and moving.*

• *Be advocates for the survey project*—be cheerleaders.

• *Symbolize the strategic change process.* Unless the members of the steering committee really believe in the process and "walk their talk," they will breed cynicism.

• *Set up an administrative apparatus* consistent with the mission and strategic change process, which also symbolizes the desired changes: "If 'people are our most important asset,' then the top Human Resources Manager should be very competent, understand the company's business, and report at a senior level where he or she can have an influence."

• *Coordinate, direct, and motivate others.*

• *Determine how to build program ideas* throughout the organization and for the long term.

• *Make heroes of employees who succeed* or who are in line with the new direction.

• *Communicate and link changes* back to the process.

Unless the steering committee members are willing to accomplish these tasks, the process will build unfulfilled expectations. Employees will spend their time resisting change rather than helping the desired change to occur.

The most common dilemma with steering committees is that committee members do not have enough time. Incorporating this process properly requires the steering committee's unflagging time and attention for at least a year. The critical question becomes: Can we afford not to do this?

A word of caution: if it is too hard to get the "right" members on the steering committee, and there are expectations to accomplish major change as a result of the process, then be very careful. Do not proceed with a less influential or less powerful group. If you can't get commitment and support now, it won't get easier later. Deal with resistance as early as possible.

CHAPTER SIX

The Survey Process

Effective employee surveys have three key components: (1) a broad level of commitment and enthusiasm for the survey process companywide, (2) a good survey design, and (3) flawless execution. Although the specifics of each step in the process may vary, depending on the needs and constraints of the organization, most projects follow these basic steps:

1. Hold a steering committee meeting
2. Conduct focus group and individual interviews
3. Review interview issues, select strategic issues to build the survey
4. Customize the survey
5. Administer the survey
6. Digitize survey data
7. Analyze reports to identify key issues
8. Present feedback to top management
9. Conduct feedback sessions with managers
10. Hold employee feedback sessions
11. Create action plans
12. Monitor progress
13. Evaluate and make modifications

This chapter will describe each of these elements in some detail.

1. Hold a Steering Committee Meeting

The survey process typically begins with a meeting of the steering committee. When the steering committee meets for the first time it helps to begin with a discussion of the roles and responsibilities of committee members, such as:

- Guide the overall project
- Give feedback when requested about survey design and architecture
- Champion projects with others throughout the process
- Help identify and negotiate potential roadblocks
- Help develop a communication plan
- Attend as many meetings as schedules permit
- Make decisions and plans with a quorum when the full group cannot be in attendance
- Support decisions made by the group
- Do not publicize outside the meetings any differences of opinion within the committee

In the initial meeting, the steering committee should establish goals and desired outcomes for the survey project, which will provide a vision for the entire project. The goals should reflect the particular circumstances of the organization, capture its character, and address the needs of the immediate situation. Here are a few examples of possible goals:

- We will develop an organizational survey to:
  —measure the effectiveness of critical business processes
  —provide valuable information for managers to help them guide the organization
  —focus on change efforts that will give the company a significant competitive advantage
  —identify the business processes that are at parity with the competition
  —provide feedback on behaviors that support or detract from critical business practices

- We will provide regular accounting of our progress on seven critical factors that will help us create a world-class organization.
- We will use employee surveys to provide quick, regular assessment of our progress on issues we consider strategically important.
- We value our employees' input and will use surveys to capture their opinions on issues important to their satisfaction and that will keep this company productive and profitable.
- We will strive to continually improve our company's culture and effectiveness. Our employee surveys will help us assess our strengths and weaknesses, and we will measure these issues regularly. We will carefully consider the results and focus our efforts on improving a few critical issues.

The goals, objectives, and vision of the survey may be short and to the point, or developed into a position paper that describes what will occur in greater detail. Often, the goals and vision will be fairly rough in the beginning. But, as the steering committee meets in future sessions, the vision should be clarified and articulated.

The committee should also develop a rough timetable for the project, at the very least deciding when the project should be completed. Starting with the completion date and working backwards, the demands of the schedule will become clear. When the timetable for the survey is clear, the committee should create a tentative schedule for its meetings during the project.

Typically, the steering committee meets to review the focus group results, finalize the survey, review the survey's administration process, review the initial results, discuss the feedback process, and work through a root-cause analysis of high-priority issues. Five plans should be created by the steering committee:

- Administration plan
- Communication plan
- Analysis plan
- Feedback plan
- Change plan

Administration plan. The chosen method of survey administration must fit the needs and characteristics of the organization. People tend to underestimate the time and effort required to administer an effective employee survey. Therefore, the steering committee should make clear assignments to each member for survey administration. Also, survey efforts will be more successful if employees are allowed to participate in the administration process.

Different administration methods, such as mandatory surveys, may yield better returns but these methods also require more effort and administrative assistance. Later in this chapter, I will discuss different administration techniques in detail. Early planning of survey administration will help avoid delays and costly mistakes.

Communication plan. One key to successful surveys is an effective and highly visible communication program. It quickly becomes evident that communication is lacking when employees receive a survey without having heard of the project. Such errors raise many questions about the purpose of the survey. An effective communication plan provides for several communications in different formats prior to a survey's administration. It also ensures that any questions raised during the survey's administration may be answered quickly. Finally, as the results begin to flow back, additional communications should outline the feedback process and discuss the overall results.

Analysis plan. The value of organizational surveys increases when analysts are able to "slice and dice" the data. Survey results provide an opportunity to evaluate results by division, department, or team and also by demographics such as position, tenure, age, gender, race, and other measures. Top management faces the problem of digesting a large amount of information in a short time. To facilitate this process, the steering committee should analyze and then summarize the results for top management. The summary should include sufficient detail to help executives understand the results without getting them caught up in too much analysis.

Feedback plan. Regardless of how good a survey is, any survey effort can fail if the feedback process is not effective. The feedback plan determines how results will be presented, who will receive the feedback, the medium for providing the feedback, and recommends how managers should share the feedback with employees. It also determines what additional materials should accompany the survey feedback to make it easier to understand and manage. The real work of the survey project begins when the data comes back.

Change plan. As a desired end result, the survey process should lead to an improved organization. If surveys are designed only to gather interesting information about employee perceptions, the process will be a failure. The steering committee should prepare an action plan to help move the survey from merely providing data to a role of fostering noticeable change.

In addition to these five plans, the steering committee should interview people to serve on focus groups, as well as select candidates for the interview process itself. Typically, each executive is interviewed individually, and a cross section of employees representing various levels, functions, and locations is interviewed for participation in focus groups. Although the number of interviews may vary, depending on the size and complexity of the organization, five to ten individual interviews and 50 to 100 people interviewed in focus groups should be sufficient. Each focus group should include about eight people.

2. Conduct Focus Group and Individual Interviews

The purpose of the focus group and individual interviews is to:

- Understand the issues that are critical to the organization's success.
- Learn the changes employees feel are most needed for the organization to be more productive and efficient.
- Introduce the survey project to employees, understand their reactions to the project, and ask their advice on making the project more successful.
- Clarify at what levels in the organization different issues occur.
- Validate employee understanding of company goals, priorities, and strategies.

Interviews generally last from 45 to 60 minutes. Focus groups should allow each member to express his or her opinions openly; too many focus group members typically prevents this. The comments from all focus groups should be compiled and analyzed by themes. The themes from the interviews should provide insight into strategic issues in the company. The interviews also provide a sense of the negative issues that will surface in survey results. Interviews also help the company recognize the slang and idioms employees use to discuss the issues.[1]

Interview questions may vary depending on the specific strategies and situations of the particular company. Interviews may include questions such as:

- What is this company's business strategy?
- What makes this company distinctive?
- How would you define "high performance" for the company?
- How would you measure success for the company?
- Who are the company's competitors?
- How is this company different from its competitors?

- In what areas does the company have an advantage?
- In what areas do our competitors have an advantage?
- What are the biggest challenges for this company in the next few years?
- What skills will be needed internally to stay competitive?
- In this company, what distinguishes those who are successful from those who are average?
- As the company grows, what do you think it should expand? (product mix, markets, distribution networks, and so forth).
- If you could change anything in this company, what would you change?

Note that the above questions focus on improving strategy and productivity rather than employee satisfaction. The frustrations of employees will generally come out in interviews regardless of what questions are asked. But by focusing on strategy and productivity the discussion will be more related to improving the business rather than keeping people content.

Here is an example of some notes from a focus group interview:

- "When we did business in the past, we presented projects to a change board and they accepted them. Now it takes months to get a project through the system. Management wants everything perfect. In the meantime, there have been tremendous change and restructuring. Most of the people are just waiting for the next relocation in a few years."

- "In this industry the way for employees to make more money is to move from one company to another. You get more money by swapping companies."

- "We have reduced our staff by 30 to 40 percent in the last few years without changing the amount of work we have to do. People feel like they are picking up a lot of extra work. Many things that were getting done are no longer getting done. What is more demoralizing is having a plan they can't respond to. We spend more time responding to day-to-day demands, many of them urgent but not important. For example, management announces there will be a meeting in two days and everyone drops everything to prepare, but the meeting was planned several weeks ago."

• "Our business strategy is to design a good product, superior to our competitors. We need products that last longer and operate better than other products. Our product is the most reliable, but once the product is delivered, our service is poor."

• "Effective marketing is critical. We need better marketing."

• "Planning is important. Things just happen around here. The highest level—instead of doing strategic or long-term planning—is more concerned with day-to-day problems. I don't see the long-term."

• "We have been given cost goals to achieve, but engineering does not see the direct link to cost targets."

3. Review Interview Issues, Select Strategic Issues to Build the Survey

The interviews conducted should ultimately result in a list of issues of critical importance to the organization in achieving its strategy, along with a fairly good prediction of the negative issues that will likely proceed from the survey data. The survey will be custom designed around these issues of critical importance.

The critical issues and probable negative feedback should be presented to the steering committee, which should seek to find solutions to these issues immediately. By generating a rough action plan before the survey, the steering committee can often clarify its questions about the negative issues. These clarification items may be included in the survey to help pinpoint the issues and ensure that action will be taken.

Any issue that goes into the survey must eventually be dealt with in the feedback meetings after the survey. Often, issues raised in interviews and in focus groups will not be addressed by the survey. Raising issues that won't be resolved will only frustrate employees and cause them to distrust the process. Too often, employee surveys include issues that executives have no time, interest, or willingness to change.

In one case, interviews in a large fast-food chain showed that employees felt very little balance in their work life, and that their jobs were too demanding. As the steering committee dealt with this issue, they acknowledged the issue but felt they could not significantly change or improve it. They believed the issue to be inherent in the job. If the issue had been placed in the survey, it almost certainly would have come back negative, and no action would be taken. The committee decided to leave the issue out of the survey. It's best to place issues in a survey that have a high probability of being addressed, and hopefully improved, in the near term.

4. Customize the Survey

Customizing an employee survey often includes these steps:

- *Step 1:* Summarize interview data into a list of concerns or issues.
- *Step 2:* Match each concern with standard survey items. Note which concerns have few or no survey items associated with them.
- *Step 3:* Generate additional survey items to measure the concerns not addressed by standard items.

Writing customized items. If the organization chooses to generate additional customized items, these items should be as valid and reliable as possible. Items are valid to the extent that they correlate with other items measuring the same or similar issues. For example, suppose a person responds "Strongly Agree" to an item, and then in another survey one year later the person responds the same way as before. The item is reliable if the person responds the same way on the post-test as on the pretest.

In another example, suppose a survey includes a fairly vague item, such as "My boss is sometimes good and sometimes bad." Suppose the team constructing this item wants to measure the managerial effectiveness of supervisors. The item probably is not valid because the people responding to the item may interpret "good" or "bad" differently. Some may view the item in terms of managerial effectiveness, while others see it from a moral or religious perspective. The item is also unreliable because the word *sometimes* is vague. Every manager is sometimes good and sometimes bad.

The best method to determine the validity or reliability of an item is to use statistical techniques on large samples of individuals with a fairly complicated instrument. Most organizations do not have the resources to conduct extensive research, and the cost of such research is often difficult to justify.

However, there are some alternatives. Organizations can select or adapt items from a database of statistically validated survey items. Another alternative is to construct items to follow a few fundamental rules. If these rules are followed, companies can have confidence in the item's validity and reliability:

• *Rule 1.* The item should be a clear and concise statement (not a question) on the issue of concern. The language used should be simple.[2]

• *Rule 2.* Items should be stated positively or negatively. But be careful: The items should not be stated too positively or too negatively. Theoretically, a good item will have a normal distribution of scores along the values scale. For example, "The XYZ Company keeps me well-informed about things I need to know" would be considered positive. But "The XYZ Company keeps me extremely well-informed about everything I need to know" would be too positive, while "The XYZ Company consistently fails to keep me informed about everything I need to know" would be too negative.

• *Rule 3.* Items should measure only one issue or problem at a time. It is easy to clutter items with additional issues or problems. For example, "The XYZ Company is slow, unresponsive, and insensitive to our needs" is measuring three different things: speed, ability to respond, and willingness to respond. A positive or negative response to the above item could be the result of any one of the conditions, or all three conditions. But the results would give no indication of the reason for the positive or negative responses. If all three conditions are important, each condition should be written as a separate item. Often, only one issue underlies such multiple conditions, and the steering committee should try to determine the core issue and construct the item based on that issue.

• *Rule 4.* After an item is created, consider the following questions:

> —If people responded very negatively or positively to this item, what would that indicate?
> —If people responded very negatively or positively to this item, would the corrective action we should take be clear?
> —Does the wording of this item correctly represent the issue or problem in the organization?

• *Rule 5.* Customized items should be tested prior to administering the survey to the whole company. Ask five or six people in the organization to answer each item and then review the responses. (A convenience sample is sufficient; a representative sample is not necessary in this case.)[3] Then ask the respondents about their personal interpretations of each item and how they felt about responding to the issue: Was the question clear? What did they understand the question to be asking? Have them explain in their own words how they understood the survey question.[4] This process usually helps the steering committee to identify poorly worded or vague items.

• *Rule 6.* Do not include too many customized items. As committees develop customized items, it is common to include too many items. Many items are created simply because someone thinks the information would be interesting. But employee surveys should ask only questions that are relevant and important to company strategy and productivity. Additional items only detract from the survey and raise employee expectations.

• *Rule 7.* Some issues or problems are better suited for a written or open-ended format than the typical multiple-response format. Written items help in the correct interpretation of survey results and help to clarify and pinpoint specific problems or issues. The major problem with open-ended items, however, is that they are difficult and time-consuming to analyze properly. Nevertheless, because of the richness of information, a few open-ended items will enhance your survey.

• *Rule 8.* Avoid highly emotional, morally charged, or leading questions.

Survey response scale. After survey items are created, associate each item with an appropriate response scale. The most common scales for employee surveys are the Likert scales, which are designed to measure attitudes and values. Likert scales associate each statement with a continuum of responses, usually varying degrees of "Agree" or "Disagree."[5]

Examples of some Likert response scales include:

• Strongly Disagree, Disagree, Neutral, Agree, Strongly Agree

- Almost Never, Rarely, Occasionally, Frequently, Almost Always
- Poor, Fair, Good, Very Good, Excellent
- No Importance, Some Importance, Moderate Importance, Great Importance, Very Great Importance
- To a Very Small Extent, To a Small Extent, To Some Extent, To a Great Extent, To a Very Great Extent
- Very Dissatisfied, Dissatisfied, Neither Satisfied nor Dissatisfied, Satisfied, Very Satisfied

Another alternative to scaling survey items is anchored scales, which are designed to "anchor" the response to a preworded item, as in the following example:

"Which best describes your development experience in this company?"

a. I have had no opportunities for development.

b. I have had very limited developmental opportunities.

c. I have had a moderate amount of developmental opportunities within my specialty.

d. I have had good opportunities for development within my specialty.

e. My developmental opportunities are the best in the industry both within and outside the company.

The advantage of anchored scales is that they are more accurate and customized to fit the issue being addressed. The disadvantage is that they are difficult to generate, and they add length and complexity to the survey. Employee surveys that include all anchored scales take much longer to complete than Likert surveys.[6] And research on the effectiveness of anchored scales versus Likert scales is inconclusive.[7] So we are left to decide which is more practical and useful.

Likert scales are generally preferred. The Likert scales make surveys easier to design and quicker to complete. By using a consistent scale for all survey items, items may be contrasted to each other to determine the percentage of agreement or disagreement. However, several critical issues arise when using Likert scales. For example, should a four-point scale or five-point scale be used? (The five-point scale typically includes a neutral response. See Figure 6.1.) And, if a five-point scale is used, should it be used throughout the survey?

5-Point Scale	4-Point Scale
1. Strongly Disagree	1. Strongly Disagree
2. Disagree	2. Disagree
3. Neither Agree Nor Disagree	3. Agree
4. Agree	4. Strongly Agree
5. Strongly Agree	

Figure 6.1: Examples of Likert scales.

The rationale for using a four-point scale is that it gets people "off the fence."[8] Respondents must either agree or disagree. Some feel that this makes the results easier to interpret. Intuitively, one would expect that those who mark Neutral on a five-point scale would be equally distributed between Agree and Disagree if plotted on a four-point scale. But, in using both scales, neutral respondents have a higher probability of marking Agree on four-point scales when the items are stated positively. So, rather than getting clearer data, four-point scales actually tend to skew the data toward the positive.

This may be due to one of several factors. First, the neutral response is a real feeling. People may feel neutral because they have had both positive and negative experiences with an item, or because the item is vague or inconsistent. Second, when people do not have the option of responding neutrally, they tend to give the benefit of the doubt to a positive response rather than a negative one. For these reasons, using a four-point scale is not recommended. For those who don't like the neutral response, it may be helpful to view a neutral response as a slightly negative response. In this sense, neutral means that the performance of the organization was not good enough to merit a positive response.

What should the label at the middle of the scale be? Consider the three Likert scales in Figure 6.2:

5-Point Scale	6-Point Scale	6-Point Scale
1. Strongly Disagree	1. Strongly Disagree	1. Strongly Disagree
2. Disagree	2. Disagree	2. Disagree
3. Undecided	3. Neither Agree Nor Disagree	3. Neutral
4. Agree	4. Agree	4. Agree
5. Strongly Agree	5. Strongly Agree	5. Strongly Agree
	6. Don't Know	6. Don't Know

Figure 6.2: Examples of neutral responses on Likert scales.

As you examine these scales, notice that there may be two very different reactions to the survey items: a neutral response (Sometimes I Agree, and Sometimes I Disagree) and a Don't Know response ("I don't understand this item," or "I have not had that experience"). Mixing the two responses can generate confusing data. Often, survey results are analyzed using their mean, or average scores. By including Don't Know and Neutral in the same average, the result can pull a negative mean toward the positive or a positive mean toward the negative, especially if there are many Don't Know responses. When instructions explicitly ask people to leave items blank if they don't know how to respond, the Don't Know is marked with even more frequency, and the percent of people marking Neutral

decreases. For these reasons, it is usually best to treat Don't
Know responses as missing data or unanswered questions. I
strongly recommend having a Don't Know or Not
Applicable response in the survey scale.

*What size of scale should be used: 9 points, 7 points, or
5 points?* Figure 6.3 provides some different examples:

5-Point Scale	7-Point Scale	9-Point Scale
1. Strongly Disagree 2. Disagree 3. Neutral 4. Agree 5. Strongly Agree	1. Strongly Disagree 2. Moderately Disagree 3. Slightly Disagree 4. Neutral 5. Slightly Agree 6. Moderately Agree 7. Strongly Agree	1. Strongly Disagree 2. 3. Disagree 4. 5. Neutral 6. 7. Agree 8. 9. Strongly Agree

Figure 6.3: Examples of 5-, 7-, and 9-point Likert scales.

Scales with too few points are generally considered to be
too coarse. On the other hand, information may be lost
when scales are too constricted. Research by Percival M.
Symonds concluded that 7-point scales were optimal. His
research was based on a statistical analysis of inter-rater reliability.[9] Later research conducted by Robert Lissitz and
Samuel Green found that much of the statistical differences
that suggested 7- or 9-point scales were more reliable was
the result of statistical artifice. They concluded that 5-point
scales would yield the same reliability.[10] In another study,
Andrew Van de Ven and Daine Ferre experimented with different scales ranging from 10 to 5 points and concluded that
the 5-point scale is the most effective. They showed that the
larger response scales made it difficult for respondents to differentiate between a "7" and an "8" on the scale.[11]

Untrained raters tend to have difficulty with larger scales, and most employees have not been trained in providing ratings. Also, many of the larger scales don't provide anchors for each point on the scale. When some employees interpret a particular point on the scale one way while others interpret the same item differently, this contributes to statistical errors and confusion. For this reason, the 5-point scale is recommended for most organizational surveys.

Customizing demographics. Demographics can group survey participants by department, location, age, sex, tenure, education, race, and other criteria. To get maximum value from survey efforts, data should be broken down and analyzed in the smallest possible groups. Unique differences or problems within specific groups will not show up in cumulative results.

For example, John Kelly reviewed the results of his company's recent organization survey. After reviewing the report for the total group, it was apparent that the company was in pretty good shape. The report showed the organization to be more positive than the norms on almost every measure. But John, a new employee, was surprised by the result. His experience in the central office with his peers was that people in the company were not satisfied and were thinking of leaving.

John then reviewed some of the demographic reports. The figures on education showed that only 15 percent of the employees who completed the survey had an undergraduate degree or higher. For the past 20 years, the company (which was in the business of delivering petroleum products) had hired truck drivers and depot managers from small farming communities. These people felt they were well-paid and had exceptional benefits. But in the last five years the company had come up against stiff competition, and faced drastic changes in the price of petroleum products.

To cope with these changes, the company had hired a group of professionals in the central office, who did everything from forecasting the price of oil to installing integrated computer systems in the branch offices. The company took pride in how it treated all employees the same, regardless of position or education. But John noticed that employees with a high school education or less were significantly more positive than the norm, while employees with undergraduate degrees or higher were significantly more negative.

Another demographic report showed that employees from the central office were more negative, though they were not as negative as the well-educated group. And, interestingly, John found that 95 percent of the employees with undergraduate and masters degrees worked at the central office. However, the managers and supervisors at the central office were very positive. (Most had been with the company for over 15 years.) The most negative demographic group in the company included employees with an undergraduate degree or higher who worked at the central office.

John reviewed the negative issues and found that these employees felt they had no chance for growth, development, or promotion. Most also felt they had very little input in company decisions. Even though the company had hired these employees to improve the company's competitiveness, company management continued to make hasty decisions and either ignored or discounted reports from the newly hired professionals. In fact, only one of the new employees had moved into management. If John had relied on the report for the total organization, he would have overlooked some valuable information for the company.

Most useful and least useful demographics. Having more demographics is not always better. Although demographics often help pinpoint negative issues in organizations, too many demographics in a survey can also create suspicion or distrust. Even though employees are told, "You will not, under any circumstances, be individually identified," they are quick to figure out when reports can be broken down into department, location, position, tenure, age, sex, and race, that they may be easily identified—especially if the survey comes in a labeled envelope with a number and barcode. One employee commented, "I'm the only female supervisor in this department. I *can* be individually identified."

The steering committee should communicate that although it is possible to identify employees, they will *not* be identified. Nevertheless, to reduce anxiety about being identified, only the most essential demographics should be asked in the survey. Some demographics are more useful than others. By "useful" I mean that a certain demographic has a higher probability of showing significant differences between groupings than others. For example, this list of possible demographic groups is prioritized according to usefulness, with 1 being the most useful and 10 the least useful:

1. Division, department, unit, group, or location
2. Position/pay group in the organization
3. Tenure
4. Age
5. Sex
6. Shift or work hours
7. Education
8. Race
9. Function (i.e., accountant, engineer, assembler)
10. Number of direct subordinates

Developing a coding scheme. Although it may seem simple to encode surveys to identify employees according to work groups, the process is often confusing and produces errors. Before helping a client develop a coding scheme, I often ask clients if the employees will recognize the work groups being listed. The response is usually, "Well, they should." This is a clue that the coding scheme won't work. Errors will likely occur in some of the following situations:

• Work group names or numbers are not well-known or recognized by employees. (Remember: Your perception may come from the fact that you know the name of your own organizational unit, but you may need to find out from other levels how employees refer to themselves to verify your perceptions.)

• Employees at lower levels of the organization refer to organizational units using different terminology than do employees at higher organizational levels.

• Those responsible for the coding scheme do not really understand the makeup of the organizational units. (The problem: These people *think* they know, but never bother to check and make sure.)

• The coding scheme is developed by someone in a hurry, who fails to review or consult with others about the scheme.

Precoding. In some surveys, organizational codes may be pre-coded on survey forms. The advantage of precoding is that, if the surveys are delivered to the appropriate employees, the technique generally produces accurate results. The disadvantage is that this method can make employees feel very suspicious. The employees are not sure whether the numbers identify their department or identify them individually.

In situations where precoding is deemed necessary but may create distrust, some organizations resort to "secret" coding schemes. For example, one company printed surveys in ten different colors and mailed them to different locations. Some clever employees found out about the coding scheme and led others to believe that certain groups were being identified. Other employees began to speculate that the encoded surveys could also identify individuals. Ultimately, the coding process created more distrust and suspicion than participation.

5. Administer the Survey

Survey administration can be a key to the overall success of change efforts because it conveys the tone and importance of the survey. Effective survey administration may use one of two different techniques: captive and noncaptive. The captive technique allows for a high degree of control. Employees attend a meeting where instructions are given, and surveys are then distributed, completed, and returned to administration personnel. In noncaptive administration, surveys are usually mailed or handed out to employees, and the employees are given time, perhaps a week, to complete and return the surveys. Consider these issues when choosing your survey administration technique:

Noncaptive Technique

1. The average return rate from noncaptive surveys is roughly 50 percent, with the range between 30 percent and 80 percent. Recently, an organization of 10,000 employees selected a sample of 1,800 to complete a survey. Considerable care was taken to ensure the sample was random. After the surveys were administered, only 52 percent were completed and returned. The care that had been taken to ensure a random selection of employees was useless because of the poor return rate. Results had to be verified at each location for accuracy, a very time-consuming process.

2. Noncaptive surveys require less involvement of those responsible for survey efforts.

3. Noncaptive techniques, in which surveys are mailed to employees' homes for completion, sometimes are viewed by employees as an attempt by management to get more work out of the employees. One employee commented, "If management thought this survey was really important, they would have provided us with the time to complete it at work. As it is, most employees have to complete the survey during their breaks, on their lunch hour, or at home in the evening."

4. Successful noncaptive surveys are always associated with excellent communication in the company. With excellent communication, employees receive advance notice that a survey will take place, managers encourage and provide time for the employees to complete and return the surveys, and finally, managers at all levels express a commitment to do something with the survey results.

Captive Technique

1. Captive techniques usually generate a 90 to 95 percent return rate. Only those on vacation, sick, or out of town miss completing the survey when it is administered.

2. Captive surveys require substantially more planning and preparation on the part of those responsible for survey efforts. All employees must be able to attend the administration session. Also, survey administration usually requires a facilitator to be present to answer questions and collect completed surveys. Inadequate planning often results in scheduling conflicts or groups that do not complete the survey.

3. Captive administration may be used as a company meeting for new communications for all employees. One large organization with plants in different locations prepared a video in which the president of the company encouraged the employees to complete surveys openly and honestly, and thanked employees for their efforts to improve the company.

4. Organizations with small units in many different locations find it impossible to use the captive technique with a facilitator at each location. However, some companies get around this problem by having a qualified employee in each location, other than the manager, act as a facilitator. If necessary, the employee facilitator can be given detailed instructions and assistance from a main facilitator. In this case, surveys are completed by each employee, sealed in envelopes, and then given back to the employee facilitator.

Captive Administration Checklist

1. *Accounting.* Get an up-to-date count of people in your organization and where they are located. Make a complete roll so you can check people off.

2. *Scheduling.* Develop a survey administration schedule, listing which groups will go to which room to take the survey, and when each group's surveys will occur. Allow adequate time to complete the survey. The average time is about 40 minutes, but allow one hour between start times for moving people in and out of the room, and for people who may take more time.

3. *Communication.* Get the word out in advance through supervisory meetings, memos, and newsletters. Make sure people know when they will take the survey and where to meet.

4. *The Room.* Arrange for a room large enough to seat each group comfortably, and make sure the room's temperature remains comfortable even when filled to capacity.

5. *Introduction.* When everyone in a group is seated, carefully explain the purpose for the survey and what goals the company hopes to achieve by conducting the survey. Also inform the groups about when results will be available and how they will be presented. Ask the respondents to complete the survey as accurately and honestly as possible, and to please raise their hands if they have any questions. Then distribute the surveys, instruct the group on how to complete it and explain what to do with it once they are finished.

6. *Questions.* Be prepared to respond to questions. In fact, before you hand out the survey, ask if the instructions were clear and if anyone has additional questions. Try not to embarrass those who ask the questions. As the employees complete the surveys, they may raise their hands. Go to them and talk with them individually. Some frequently asked questions include:

- If I don't have knowledge or an opinion about an item in the survey, how should I respond?
- If I don't understand a question, how should I respond?
- When the survey says "in this organization," what does the word *organization* refer to? Is it my department or the organization as a whole?
- What does "management" refer to? Is it my boss, company management in general, or senior executives?

7. *The Box.* Provide a safe place to collect completed surveys. Often, people feel anxious about having their personal comments read by others in the organization. Also, those who administer the survey should be perceived as "safe and trustworthy" by employees.

8. *Keep Track.* Keep an up-to-date roll of who has completed a survey and who is out of town, sick, or otherwise unable to attend the administration session.

9. *Follow Up.* Deliver a copy of the survey to those who were absent and provide a simple method for them to return the survey.

10. *Processing.* Deliver completed surveys to the data processing center using the fastest possible courier service. If you conducted administration sessions in multiple locations, make sure you mark each box with a number that corresponds to the specific location of the survey sessions and, if necessary, the particular customized surveys administered at that location. If a box is lost, you will know which one is lost.[12]

Administration suggestions. During the administration, potential mistakes may be avoided by taking the following steps:

- *Send letters or announcements to all employees informing them of the survey and its purpose.* Make sure they understand that they will not be individually identified.

- *If surveys are mailed, inform the employees of the date by which surveys are to be returned on the "Instructions" page.* One week from the date of receipt is a good target.
- *Distribute the survey to each person in the organization.* Surveys may be distributed through interoffice mail or handed out in group meetings.
- *If a noncaptive approach is chosen, provide time for everyone to take the survey during working hours.* This will make it easier for employees to complete it and will improve the survey's return rate. In a plant location, you might schedule specific times for employees to complete the survey since uncoordinated shutdowns may cause difficulties.

Michael Roberson and Eric Sundstrom found that two issues in the design of surveys improved return rates. By listing items of greater concern to the employees as the first items in the survey, return rates improved, perhaps because the survey items were of interest to employees. Also, placing questions relating to demographics in the back of the survey rather than in the front leads to an increase in survey return rates.[13]

Network Survey Administration. Computer networks and Internet technology have created new options for employee survey administration. Organizations that have their employees connected via computer may now administer their surveys through e-mail, the Internet, intranets, or even through telephony. Rather than receiving surveys in your desktop in-box or in a meeting room, you can receive surveys through e-mail. The e-mail message typically asks for your participation and invites you to open an attachment. You respond to the questions using your mouse or various keys on your keyboard. The process saves everyone time, and it saves the company money in faster data collection and analysis.[14]

Many organizations are not quite technically capable—not all employees have computer access, different computer systems have no common interface, or employees are not educated on how to use new technology—or perhaps they are hesitant to use new technology. However, those who have tried the new technologies in conducting employee surveys have generally been pleased with the results.

However, new technology has created other problems for surveys. Most employees believe they can be easily identified from their computer. A recent news article reported that a 16-year-old boy in Australia posted a suicide note on a web page. Although the teenager was not serious, within one day his exact location had been pinpointed. E-mail messages generally provide details of where they originated and how they are sent to the recipient.

Some companies who have access to such technology still choose to use a paper survey method because the employees trust it more. Business intranets are generally more secure than Internet connections. Employees may feel more confident in taking surveys administered via a secure intranet. In the meantime, the security options available to browsers are improving daily, which may make the confidentiality concern obsolete.

Technological competence poses another problem in using new technology for employee surveys. In a large high-tech company I visited, I found out that the top 100 executives all had a particular e-mail software installed on their desktop computers. But, after one year, only three had attempted to use the program. In another company, the top executive responded to his e-mail messages by having his administrative assistant print out all his messages. He would then write notes on the messages, and his assistant would type his notes into the e-mails and return the responses to senders. Those who have had little or no experience with computers may be much more comfortable completing surveys by hand.

Despite these problems, they are all minor and short-term. The Internet and intranets are wonderful solutions for collecting and processing survey data. Paper surveys will always exist, but the bulk of survey research in the future will likely be done via computer networks.

6. Digitize Survey Data

Once surveys are completed, all numeric and written comment data is entered into a computer-readable, or digitized, medium. Techniques for digitizing data include hand entry, scanning, telephony, and computer networks. Each method has tradeoffs. And, although efficiency and speed may be important, total accuracy in the data is critical. Hand entry requires verification. Scanning requires quality-checking. The credibility of a survey may be totally undermined by a small inaccuracy in the data. Once an error is reported in the results, employees start to distrust everything presented in the survey feedback.

7. Analyze Reports to Identify Key Issues

Survey data provides a great opportunity to analyze the organization. Groups may be compared to other groups, issues may be analyzed by demographics, and correlations may be made between items to identify how the variables affect each other. With the right software, the capacity to produce reports and analysis soon outpaces our capacity to capture and summarize those results into a simple story. With piles of feedback reports, getting lost in the "forest" can be easy. To avoid this, the steering committee needs a good analysis plan. Although each analysis plan should be unique, having a simple map to get you out of the "forest" can be helpful.

Return rates. Look at the population the survey represents and compare it to the number of surveys returned. Although it may be possible to achieve a 100 percent return rate, rates typically come in between 60 and 80 percent, and occasionally lower. A good return rate indicates that you have done a good job of setting up the survey and communicating to the employees. It also shows strong commitment in the company to improving the organization. A low return rate may indicate either resistance or apathy toward the survey.

However, survey results may or may not accurately reflect opinions of the whole group. If the process of completing or not completing the survey were a random process, then a 40 to 50 percent return rate would be expected. But if the process of returning the survey involves some bias (such as, only the negative people responded or only the positive people responded), then results will not be representative.

For demographic groups with low return rates, a sample of those who did not complete the survey should be interviewed to find out the reasons for not responding. This should provide clues about whether the results have a positive or negative bias. Most often, the process of not returning surveys is random and generally results from poor up-front communication and setup. If you have a low return rate, it is usually best to summarize the results and then verify the conclusion in the feedback process within groups.

Overall scores. Most survey results average all appropriate items in the survey into an overall score. The scores provide a simple but accurate way of determining the general climate of a group, demographic, or the whole company.

Although the overall scores are often displayed as a mean, or average score, mean scores are not generally well-understood. For example, if management says the employees had an overall mean score of 2.5, while 60 percent of the employees responded negatively in the survey, the negativity of the employees is buried in the vague and confusing mean number.

Demographics. Overall scores may be used with other results:

- Total group results
- Comparison of the total group to norms
- Comparison of divisions, departments, or locations within the total group
- Comparison of demographic results with the total group

Survey categories. While overall scores provide a general perspective on how groups compare to each other, they do not indicate which categories are more positive or more negative. Compare the various survey categories to each other. Typically, some categories will be substantially more positive or negative than others.

Identifying strengths and weaknesses. Starting with survey categories and moving to specific survey items, the strengths of the organization may be identified. Typically, strengths are very positive (over 70 percent positive) and are backed with written comments that confirm the positive conclusion. But a company's strengths are not always identified within established categories in the survey. Occasionally, a set of positive items cuts across several categories.

Weaknesses are identified by the most negative items. Items are considered negative when 25 percent or less responds positively. Typically, negative items are not as negative as positive items are positive. As with strengths, weaknesses occasionally cut across survey categories.

Issues that leverage other issues. The descriptive statistics (mean scores, ranges, and deviations) present a one-dimensional view of survey results. Each dimension in survey data is linked to the total result, as well as to the other dimensions. Correlations, however, provide a multidimensional view of the results. For issues that are negative, a correlation analysis can provide insight into what drives the result. For example, a refinery measured its progress on several key initiatives. Although employees saw progress on a few issues, the results also showed that the employees felt little progress had been made overall. A correlation analysis showed the following items to be highly correlated with the overall score:

- "I believe our management does a good job of resolving problems before they become crises."
- "This company keeps the employees well-informed about the reasons for changes and how those changes will affect the employees."
- "I trust that management will report information honestly to employees."
- "This company organizes work so that I am able to maximize my productivity and effectiveness."
- "Management will not allow the pressures of the moment to influence actions and decisions that go against their stated commitments and values."
- "Groups responsible for decision-making work hard to ensure that they identify, gather, integrate, and share all relevant information."

The list provided an excellent way for people to see the issues that stood in the way of the company's progress. Letting problems go too long without being resolved, not communicating changes when they occurred, lack of trust in the information communicated, poor organization and information gathering prior to decisions, and not keeping commitments—all contributed to the end result: that the employees saw very little progress on the key initiatives. The items most closely correlated to the overall result leveraged the perception of progress for the employees. So, for the employees to see progress on the actual goals, they needed to see progress in these other areas first. Including a correlation analysis in an executive summary is an effective way to demonstrate how such issues can be resolved.

Written comment themes. Written comments represent a rich source of data, providing depth and insight that numbers alone won't allow. What makes written comments confusing is that they lack consistency, they usually cover broad and often vague ground, and very few survey respondents provide them. In a typical survey, about 25 percent of the respondents do not write in any comments. When employees do write comments, they comment on things that are important or significant to them personally. But, because they may comment on such a wide variety of issues, the size of a significant positive or negative comment can be as low as 10 percent of the respondents.

Comments, however, have the power to persuade. In one case, as I worked with a group of executives, we uncovered some very compelling data in the numbers. The executives acknowledged the data but seemed unaffected. Later, as we reviewed the written comments, some of which described sobering personal circumstances, the executives suddenly "got it." The influence of the comments was noticeably powerful.

Comments can also be dangerous. Often, the first thing that pops into a manager's head when reading anonymous employee comments is "I wonder who wrote this." And, given the ability of the company to identify the respondent, care must be taken in reviewing survey data, both numerical and written responses, to prevent such lapses in judgment from hurting the credibility of the survey. In some cases, it would be best to only allow written comments to be reviewed at high levels by those who do not work directly with the respondents.

Recommended actions. In any analysis, it is important to formulate some conclusions and outline a process for taking action. Remember that other people will generally be responsible for making the changes. The analysis of data should not preclude involvement by executives in formulating the conclusions and deciding on recommended actions.

8. Present Feedback to Top Management

The feedback process begins with a top management feedback session, an important place to begin. For feedback sessions to be effective, consider these suggestions:

• *Set aside enough time.* Feedback sessions typically require three to four hours. Although it is possible to conduct the session in less time, when this happens executives often leave the meeting with many questions (and possibly some resistance).

• *Make sure the right people attend.* This first group should not be too large, and a mixed group can create an atmosphere that feels less open. Also, it is fair to allow top management the opportunity to review the results with enough time to consider the messages and implications of the data before being put on the spot to commit to changes.

• *Include sufficient detail* to help executives understand the data, but not so much as to confuse or complicate the presentation.

• *Avoid making this a winner/loser session.* Everyone can "win" in the survey process if the result will be a more competitive and productive company.

• *Executives sometimes react defensively.* They may need time to understand where the data is coming from and what it means to them.

• *Work toward specific outcomes in the meeting.* Unless they are well-planned, feedback sessions with top management can end without specific next steps. Make sure the executives know what is recommended to be done next as a result of the survey data.

• *Don't expect too much from one feedback session.* Often, feedback sessions are set up in which executives must review survey results, make decisions on action items, and generate an action plan. But accomplishing all of this in one meeting may be unrealistic. When adequate time is not available, detailed action plans should be deferred to the next steering committee meeting. Frequently, executives will simply instruct others to make the necessary changes. (Action plans are covered in greater detail in Chapter 8 on Root-Cause Analysis.)

9. Conduct Feedback Sessions with Managers

The main purpose of an employee survey is to stimulate change. If the change plan only covers companywide initiatives, then all the pressure is on top management to carry out the plan. But, if survey data is driven down the organization and provided to departments and work groups, then changes can occur at multiple levels in the organization. Changes that occur in work groups have more personal significance than broad organizational initiatives. It's a bit like taxes: If you are taxed for new road construction but you never see improvements in your own neighborhood, you may feel your tax money is not well spent.

Driving survey data down the organization is a useful way to get more change out of survey efforts. It only works, however, if the managers and supervisors in the organization are prepared to share survey results and make meaningful changes. To maximize the change effort, managers must:

- Clearly understand the survey results
- Have strong interpersonal skills
- Trust the survey process
- Receive support materials

Managers must clearly understand the survey results. The most important element in a change process is for managers and supervisors at all levels to thoroughly understand the overall survey results and their individual data. Sharing the executive summary with managers and supervisors is helpful, since the summary includes clear details and concise recommendations for improvement. The issues identified in the executive summary may be similar for many work groups. Also, the summary provides a helpful model for how to present the survey data.

Managers and supervisors should also receive the results for their work groups. Work group results may be created for groups as small as three to five employees. The results should provide a basic summary of data for the group compared to norms in the company.

Managers must have strong interpersonal skills. For effective feedback meetings further down the company, managers and supervisors should be proficient in:

- Holding collaborative meetings
- Listening effectively
- Discussing sensitive issues without becoming defensive
- Presenting data in a nonthreatening, problem-solving approach
- Solving problems effectively
- Planning effectively

Managers must trust the survey process. Managers should feel confident that they are not getting "caught" by the survey results, and that they will be supported by management in making their changes. Managers and supervisors should be judged on what they do with their results, not on how positively or negatively results come out in the feedback report.

Managers must receive support materials. Managers and supervisors need support materials to help them make the feedback process easier. The executive summary, interpretation guides, action planning guides, and resource guides are all tools that will make the process work better.

10. Employee Feedback Sessions

After the top management and manager feedback sessions, it would be easy to believe that the majority of work has been done in the feedback process. But the reality is that the process has only just started. Employees who take the time and effort to complete surveys want to understand the results from their group, as well as how they compare to the total company. Feedback sessions include reviewing survey results, clarifying issues, and soliciting employee suggestions on the results of the survey.

11. Create Action Plans

Based on all the information from the survey, action plans need to be developed. Systematic changes over time will lead to an improved work climate. John Hinrichs suggests a simple structure for the topics that should be covered in action plans: objectives, resources needed, implementation steps, responsibilities, and a timetable.[15] The largest single mistake in creating action plans is trying to accomplish too much rather than focusing on a few strategic changes. Action plans should be developed at both the company (or division) level and the work group level. The steering committee is in charge of the company action plans, reviewing the results of the survey and additional information gathered in feedback sessions.

Company action plans must (1) get to the root-cause of problems and (2) assign an influential top executive the responsibility for making specific changes. Work group action plans are usually easier to create. But since work groups have so many other competing demands, I strongly recommend that they promptly review the survey results and then focus on one issue for change. Most managers will feel optimistic that they can make at least one significant change in the next year. By having action plans at the work-group level, employees gain a clearer sense that the survey is causing change.

In a recent survey, employees were asked their opinion on three items related to their previous survey:

- My work group is working to make meaningful changes based on the results of last year's survey.

- My work group was successful in improving an issue identified by last year's survey.
- This organization has addressed the companywide issues identified by last year's survey.

Figure 6.4 shows the results for the third item. It compares "when work group results were not reviewed and action *was not* taken" with "when work group results were reviewed and action *was* taken." The results clearly showed that when work group actions were taken, 86 percent of the employees responded positively about the companywide actions being accomplished, but when work group feedback did not occur and actions were not taken at the work group level, only 6 percent of the employees felt the organization had addressed companywide issues.

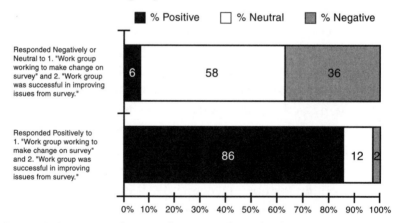

Figure 6.4: Comparison of actions taken or not taken on work group results.

Work group feedback and actions provide people with a definite sense that something is resulting from survey efforts. Company efforts are less personal and may not be noticed or remembered by work group members.

12. Monitor Progress

An employee survey is an event. When an event is over, it is often easy to forget the action items and start thinking about the next event. Effective action plans should include ways to remind people about action items and commitments, as well as updates on the progress and results—especially when linked to the survey. Too often, employees forget why actions are being taken. At the work group level, action plans can also be included in individual development plans for managers or supervisors who are reviewed quarterly or twice a year. Each work group should also consider ways to monitor their own progress on action items.

13. Evaluate and Make Modifications

At the conclusion of the survey effort, evaluate the survey items (as well as the entire project) to consider modifications for the next survey. Many times, organizations ask for surveys with as few items as possible so they can predict results more accurately. This efficiency can also be accomplished in a thorough analysis of survey items and a validation of the results. Management and employee commitment in the survey process should also be reviewed.

Statistically evaluating employee surveys. Each year after the survey is collected and analyzed, it ought to be examined statistically. Think of this review as a regular "tune up" for the survey. Using the data, it will be simple to find ways to make the survey more effective, efficient, and valid.

Highest and lowest scoring items. This analysis is designed to uncover items that may have been too difficult or too easy, thereby adding little additional insight into employee opinions. An analysis of one survey showed the following as the most positive item in a survey:

> "I feel responsible for the successful accomplishment of my work."

The average score on this item was 4.57. And 95 percent of all responses were positive while only 2 percent were negative. The item itself was not the problem. It was not biased, nor did it creating misunderstandings. But it did not add any insight either. And, though the item did not hurt the survey, the survey would have been more efficient without it. Not all positive items should be dropped. Sometimes positive items continue to reinforce company values and principles that are critical to success.

Frequency distributions and descriptive statistics (mean, standard deviation, skew, and kurtosis). The graphic distribution of an item also helps determine its effectiveness. The normal distribution is symmetrical and has no skew (or rather, a skew that equals zero) and no kurtosis (or a kurtosis static value of zero). "Skew" measures the asymmetry of a distribution. A distribution that is significantly skewed toward the positive has a long right tail. A distribution that is significantly skewed toward the negative has a long left tail. "Kurtosis" measures the extent to which data cluster around a central point. Positive kurtosis indicates that observations cluster more and have longer tails than those in the normal distribution, while negative kurtosis indicates that observations cluster less and have shorter tails.

Figure 6.5, a histogram, shows the frequency of response to values on a survey scale of 1 to 5, and it shows an item with high skew and positive kurtosis. The normal curve is superimposed over the histogram bars.

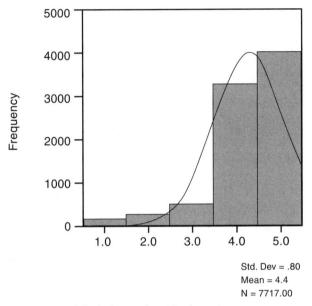

Std. Dev = .80
Mean = 4.4
N = 7717.00

Figure 6.5: An item with high skew and positive kurtosis.

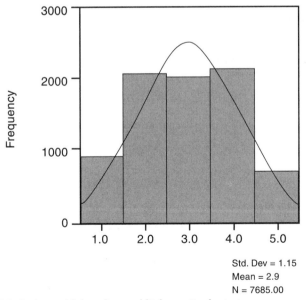

Std. Dev = 1.15
Mean = 2.9
N = 7685.00

Figure 6.6: An item with low skew and high negative kurtosis.

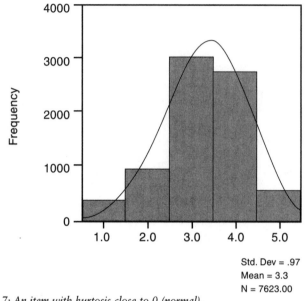

Figure 6.7: An item with kurtosis close to 0 (normal).

Missing and neutral values. An excellent indicator of a poor item is one that contains a high percentage of missing values. Missing values indicate that the item was either confusing or difficult to answer. Sometimes, items with a high percentage of missing values can provide insight into organizational problems and concerns. For example, one organization included this item in its survey:

> "I understand where this company is going in the future."

About 11 percent of the responses were missing, and 20 percent marked "Neither Agree nor Disagree." The percentage of missing or neutral data indicated poor communication to employees concerning the company's strategy and direction.

At other times, a high percentage of missing values may point out items that are not as effective as they could be. For example, this item had a high percentage of missing data:

> "I get regular feedback from external customers
> on how well I am meeting their needs."

In the organization that asked this question, few employees had regular contact with customers. So, although this item might be appropriate in some organizations, it was not appropriate in this company.

Factor analysis. A factor analysis provides a statistical view of how survey items cluster. One organization that had conducted a survey for several years performed a factor analysis on its survey items and found that it could simplify its survey. They found several items, included in different categories, that clustered around each other in the factor analysis. Upon further inspection, the items were found to be similar enough that several could be eliminated. This made the survey more efficient without losing critical information.

Reliability analysis. A reliability analysis is a statistical procedure that allows you to study the effectiveness of survey items within each category.[16] The procedure calculates several common measures of effectiveness and the relationship between survey items. With reliability analysis, you can determine the extent to which items in your questionnaire are related to each other. You can also compile an overall index of the repeatability or internal consistency of the scale as a whole, and identify problem items that should be excluded from the category.

Validation analysis. Validation analysis involves testing the survey's ability to predict organizational performance and effectiveness. A valid survey should be able to distinguish high-performing and low-performing groups. It should also predict, when conditions are right, several other measures of organizational effectiveness.

One validation analysis compared the results from 30 groups in a company survey against three measures of organizational effectiveness. An index was created of the 50 items in the survey that were the most effective in predicting organizational effectiveness scores. Figures 6.8 through 6.10 show the mean differences from groups scoring high, medium, and low on the survey compared to the results on each of the three organizational effectiveness measures.

Figure 6.8 demonstrates that the groups with higher survey scores had significantly lower voluntary turnover.

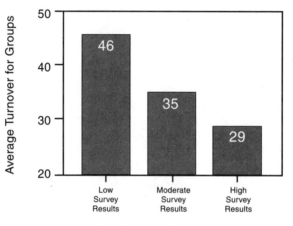

50 Item Predictive Index

Figure 6.8: Comparison of voluntary turnover by survey results.

Figure 6.9 shows substantial improvement in profitability for groups with higher scores on the survey.

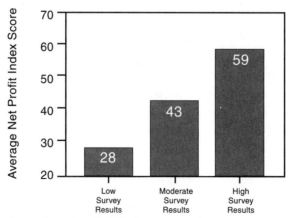

Figure 6.9: Comparison of profitability by survey results.

Figure 6.10 shows that groups with higher survey scores also have higher customer satisfaction scores. With this analysis the company was able to determine which survey items were most effective at predicting organizational effectiveness. The validation also gave both managers and employees greater confidence in the survey.

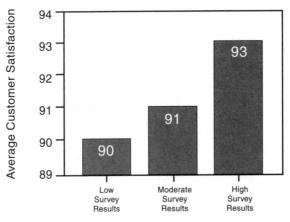

Figure 6.10: Comparison of customer satisfaction by survey results.

Evaluating the survey process. The following list is a potential problem analysis, which can serve as a guide to help you identify weak aspects in your survey process:

1. Failure to generate commitment or interest in doing a survey from a majority of the top managers that will be involved in the survey.

2. Failure to generate commitment or interest in doing a survey from a majority of the employees involved in the survey.

3. Failure to link the survey to business needs.

4. Failure to communicate to employees the purpose of the survey and its objective.

5. Failure to identify and resolve issues associated with those who see survey data, including how data will be managed, avoiding distrust between management and employees or between different departments in the organization.

6. Failure to identify appropriate groupings prior to survey administration. Groups cannot be created after administration. If data needs to be broken out by department and you fail to ask for that demographic, there is no way to create that variable post hoc.

7. Failure to administer surveys to appropriate employees because:

    a. Employees were not scheduled to attend administration sessions.

    b. Employees who were supposed to be mailed surveys were not on the mailing list.

    c. Employees who were sick or on vacation were not given an opportunity to complete the surveys.

8. Failure to perform accurate accounting of surveys after administration.

9. Failure to ship surveys to the data processing company using a secure, efficient service.

10. Failure to communicate to the data processing company how data should be analyzed.

11. Failure to sufficiently analyze survey data. Survey data was skimmed over and the real underlying problems were never understood or addressed.

12. Failure of managers to allocate sufficient time to review and understand survey results.

13. Failure of managers to share survey results with employees.

14. Failure of managers to create or follow an action plan.

15. Failure of managers to involve employees who would effect changes in the organization.

16. Failure of action plans to be specific and realistic.

17. Failure to follow up on action plans.

Conclusions

This chapter has presented a process for conducting employee surveys. Not every survey needs to follow every step, but each step can be useful. And although it is always important to be creative, survey processes that omit these steps have problems and return suboptimal results. A key to making any process work effectively is to fit this general process to the specific needs of your organization.

Notes to Chapter Six

1. Allen I. Kraut and Allen J. Kraut, *Organizational Surveys: Tools for Assessment and Change*, San Francisco, CA: Jossey-Bass, 1996, 161, 164, 166.

2. Excellent guides to help with the wording of survey items are contained in Stanley L. Payne, *The Art of Asking Questions,* Princeton, NJ: Princeton University Press, 1951; Howard Schuman and Stanley Presser, *Questions and Answers in Attitude Surveys: Experiments in Question Form, Wording, and Context,* New York: Academic Press, 1981; and Seymour Sudman and Norman M. Bradburn, *Asking Questions: A Practical Guide to Questionnaire Design*, San Francisco, CA: Jossey-Bass, 1982.

3. Kraut and Kraut, *Organizational Surveys*, 161, 164, 166.

4. William A. Belson, B. L. Millerson, and Peter J. Didcott, *The Development of a Procedure for Eliciting Information from Boys about the Nature and Extent of their Stealing.* London: Survey Research Centre, London School of Economics and Political Science, 1968.

5. Rensis Likert, "A Technique for Measurement of Attitude." *Archives of Psychology* (1932), 140. Anne Anastasi. *Psychological Testing*, 5th edition, New York: Macmillan, 1982. Warren S. Torgerson, *Theory and Methods of Scaling*, New York: Wiley & Sons, 1958.

6. Norbert F. Elbert, Carol Saunders, and Jason Schweizer, "The Role of Practicality in the Choice of Instructor Rating Methods," *Journal of Experimental Education* 51 (1983), 3:114-21.

7. Kafry Jacobs and Zedeck Jacobs, "Expectation of Behaviorally Anchored Rating Scales," *Personnel Psychology* 33 (1980), 3:595-640.

8. Kraut and Kraut, *Organizational Surveys*, 161, 164, 166.

9. Percival M. Symonds, "On the Loss of Reliability in Ratings Due to Coarseness of the Scale." *Journal of Experimental Psychology* (December 1924), 7:456-61.

10. Robert W. Lissitz and Samuel B. Green, "Effects of the Number of Scale Points on Reliability: A Monte Carlo Approach." *Journal of Applied Psychology* 60 (February 1975), 1:10-13.

11. Andrew H. Van de Ven and Daine L. Ferre, *Measuring and Assessing Organizations*. New York: Wiley & Sons, 1980.

12. For additional information on developing and conducting effective employee surveys, please contact Novations Group, Inc., at (801) 375-7525.

13. Michael T. Roberson and Eric Sundstrom, "Questionnaire Design, Return Rates, and Response Favorableness in an Employee Attitude Questionnaire." *Journal of Applied Psychology* 75 (1990), 3:354-57.

14. For an example of Internet-based surveys, please visit **http://surveys.novations.com.** After typing in the password, "ORGDEMO" a form resembling a paper survey comes into view. You respond to survey items by clicking your mouse.

15. Kraut and Kraut, *Organizational Surveys*, 161, 164, 166.

16. SPSS Professional Statistics 8.0 (Copyright 1997 SPSS, Inc.), Chicago, IL., 359.

CHAPTER SEVEN

Trends in Employee Survey Data

A large plant conducted an employee survey, which contained approximately 70 items. Each employee was given the opportunity to participate. Later, members of the steering committee prepared an index, which averaged each of the 70 items and provided an overall perspective of how the employees scored on the survey. The members reviewed the results by position, using the chart in Figure 7.1:

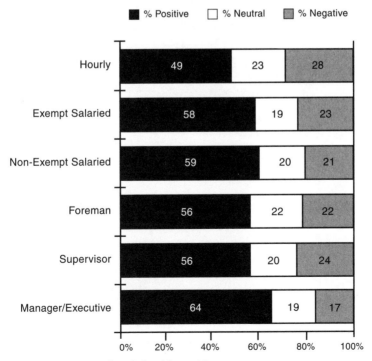

Figure 7.1: Survey results tabulated by position.

When the members of the steering committee saw these results, they reasoned that the small differences between nonexempt salaried employees, foremen, and supervisors indicated a positive trend. They felt the data reflected a level playing field between the employees at each of the three levels. Then the steering committee was shown the norms for several different organizational tiers. Figure 7.2 shows the norms:

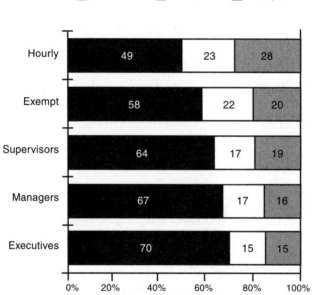

Figure 7.2: Survey norms for different organizational tiers.

Consistently in employee surveys, each organizational tier tends to view things more positively, and less negatively, than the tier below.

When the steering committee members considered the data in light of the norms, they began to understand why their results might be skewed. Recently, supervisors in the organization had been frustrated and discouraged. The results indicated that the supervisors had responded slightly more negatively than the foremen. In turn, the foremen were slightly more negative than the nonexempt salaried employees. Thus, what had initially seemed to be a positive trend was in fact a substantial issue.

Most employee survey data reflects norms, but an understanding of how those norms look and some basic trends will help you know when your results are unusual. This chapter will review some of the norms and trends that are common throughout a majority of organizations. It will also review different analytical techniques used to compare employee surveys against those norms and trends, and to understand the implications of your data.

Satisfaction Index

To illustrate typical survey trends, I will show the results from a typical satisfaction index. The four basic items of the index are:

In general . . .
I am satisfied with my current job.
I am satisfied with my immediate manager.
I am satisfied with the management of this division.
I am satisfied with the organization as a place to work.

Respondents are to indicate the degree of satisfaction by indicating one of the following for each statement:
Strongly Agree
Agree
Neutral
Disagree
Strongly Disagree
Don't Know

First, the Don't Know responses were eliminated from the analysis. Then a data set was assembled, consisting of responses from 1,154 groups in 20 different companies.

The results were analyzed by combining the Strongly Agree with the Agree responses and the Strongly Disagree with the Disagree responses. Figure 7.3 depicts the results:

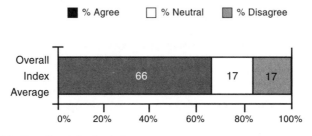

Figure 7.3: Overall satisfaction index.

In this index, 17 percent of the responses were marked Disagree or Strongly Disagree, while 66 percent were marked Agree or Strongly Agree. This represents the average of all groups in the data set. The range of Agree and Disagree responses helps in understanding the variety of responses.

In Figure 7.4, a considerable range is found between the top and bottom quartiles.

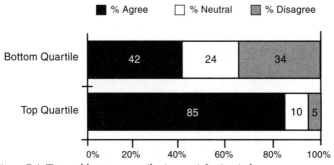

Figure 7.4: Top and bottom quartiles in a satisfaction index.

The histogram in Figure 7.5 shows the frequency of groups by the percentage of Agree or Strongly Agree responses. In this case, the scores on the graph represent group totals. The group may have been as small as a work group or as large as the whole company. Note that the distribution of scores is fairly normal, although skewed slightly to the right.

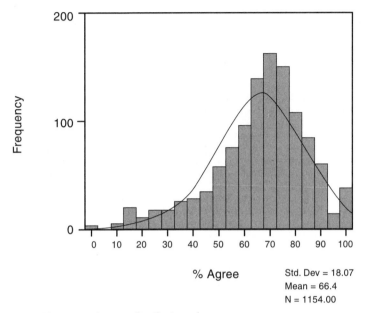

Figure 7.5: Histogram showing distribution of groups.

Demographic Trends

When employee survey data is examined using demographics, differences are often found in the results of different groups. These demographic groups typically include position, gender, race, tenure, age, and education. Although each organization may be unique in terms of the differences between these various groups, there are some consistent trends. The following section shows results for the total data set compared with results from organizations that demonstrated some unique differences in demographics.

Position. As indicated previously, executives and managers are typically more positive than professionals or front-line workers. These findings are consistent in most organizations. Figure 7.6 shows the results for the satisfac-

tion index by position averaged across the various companies in the data base.

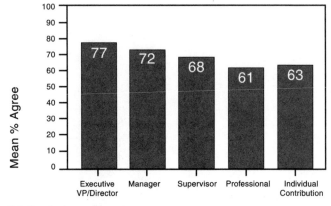

Figure 7.6: Results by position.

Gender. Male and female respondents generally show few
differences with regard to overall satisfaction (see Figure 7.7).
However, within some organizations, specific items may
show striking differences in how men and women respond.
These items reflect specific issues related to the difficulties of
managing diversity within an organization.

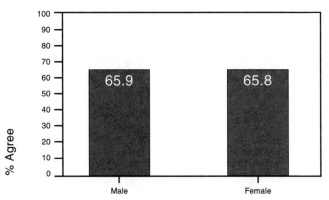

Figure 7.7: Results by gender.

Men and women do not always respond in the same way. For example, one organization conducted a survey that sharply contrasted the results for men and women. The data in Figure 7.8 was found to be much more positive for men than for women.

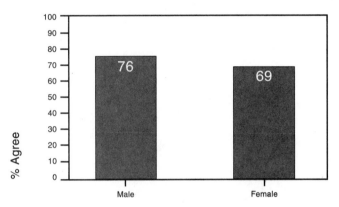

Figure 7.8: Credit given to people who contribute, comparing men and women.

The men in this organization were more likely to be given credit for contributions. On another item, which evaluated the consistency of advancement criteria (shown in Figure 7.9), the women responded significantly more positively than the men.

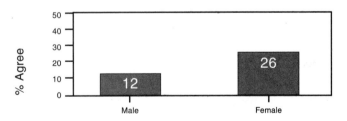

Figure 7.9: Consistency of advancement criteria, comparing men and women.

Tenure. The tenure curve is typically higher at both ends and lower in the middle (see Figure 7.10). The curve indicates that employees tend to be very positive soon after joining a company and just before retiring, but they tend to be more negative between those times. A few years after joining this organization, the employees began to recognize some of the difficulties in career progression and internal company politics. Sometimes the tenure curve correlates with mid-life crisis. The results from the overall satisfaction index are not extremely pronounced.

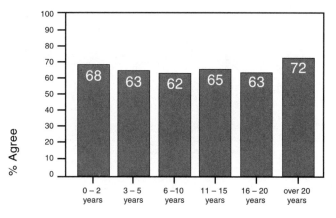

Figure 7.10: Results by tenure.

Figure 7.11 shows the results for one organization. Note that this curve is more pronounced, showing greater differentiation at the tails of the graph.

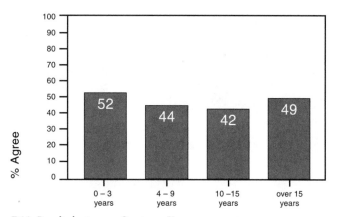

Figure 7.11: Results by tenure, Company X.

Occasionally, companies will have results that differ from norms. A flat tenure curve is not necessarily bad. In fact, it may signal a work environment that keeps people happy as they go along, rather than showing greater satisfaction at the beginning or end of one's career.

Education. Figure 7.12 shows the results for education. The education curve is similar to that of tenure (high at the ends and lower in the middle).

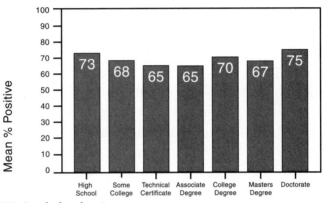

Figure 7.12: Results by education.

Race. The norms for results by race indicate that minorities tend to be more positive than nonminorities. This trend is often similar to the gender analysis, but there are some items where minorities respond substantially more negatively or positively.

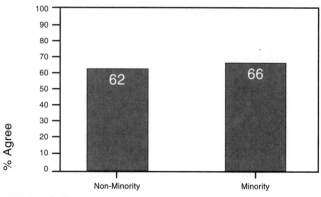

Figure 7.13: Results by race.

Impact Analysis

Another analysis technique is impact analysis, which correlates statistics to help in understanding relationships between different indices and survey items. Examining a set of approximately 100,000 respondents from multiple organizations yielded the following set of items as the most negative in the survey:

Most Negative Survey Items:

- Job assignments tend to be given based on who can do the job rather than on who needs new growth and development opportunities.
- Most work units in the division could be significantly more productive than they are.
- Decisions by management appear to favor short-term results at the expense of long-term objectives.
- There is too much inefficiency/waste in this organization.
- The way work is assigned frequently leads to poor collaboration between work groups.
- I could personally be more effective if I had better access to up-to-date equipment.
- The only way people in this organization can get ahead is to go into management.

- Once job assignments are made, people tend to get stuck in them.
- I have adequate information about what our competition is doing to enable me to do my job effectively.

By correlating each of the items in the survey with the satisfaction index, we discover the association of each item with overall satisfaction. As presented earlier in the chapter, the following items compose the satisfaction index:

Generally . . .

I am satisfied with my current job.

I am satisfied with my immediate manager.

I am satisfied with the management of this division.

I am satisfied with the organization as a place to work.

The following lists the items with the highest correlation to the satisfaction index:

High-Impact Items on Overall Satisfaction

- I am proud to be identified with the goals of this organization.
- The organization's management keeps its commitments to employees.
- My immediate manager encourages people in this work group to care about and strive for excellent performance.
- I can trust my immediate manager to be honest with me.
- My immediate manager listens openly to new ideas.
- Respect for the individual is reflected in most management decisions and actions.
- The organization reports information honestly to its employees.
- I have confidence in the judgment and management abilities of my immediate manager.

- Compared to other companies I am aware of, this organization affords the kinds of job opportunities I want.
- I have adequate opportunity for individual growth and career development in this organization.

High correlation indicates a strong relationship between the satisfaction index score and the score of an individual item. Figure 7.14 demonstrates the relationship on a low-impact item by breaking the overall satisfaction scores into high, medium, and low scoring groups and evaluating the percent of positive responses.

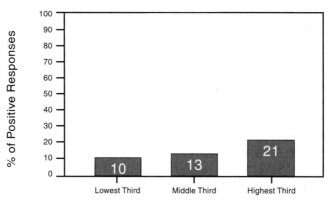

Figure 7.14: Results from a low-impact item.

The graph shows the results for the item: "Job assignments tend to be given based on who can do the job rather than on who needs new growth and development opportunities." The correlation between this item and the overall satisfaction index is .20. Note that the graph does show a slight trend, such that the most positive group in the satisfaction index was slightly more positive, and the most negative group was slightly more negative. This graph demonstrates that this item is about as negative for the group of people who have low satisfaction as it is for the group with high satisfaction.

The next chart, Figure 7.15, shows the results for the item with the highest impact score.

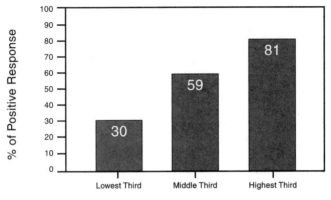

Figure 7.15: Results from a high-impact item.

The correlation is .57 for the item that reads: "I can trust my immediate manager to be honest with me." Note how the graph demonstrates the profound nature of the relationship: 81 percent of the employees with high overall satisfaction scores agreed or strongly agreed that their immediate managers would be honest with them. However, only 30 percent of those with low overall satisfaction scores agreed or strongly agreed that their immediate managers would be honest with them.

It appears from Figure 7.15 that the honesty of the immediate manager, rather than whether job assignments are given based on who can do the best job, has the most influence over a person's feeling of satisfaction at the company. If one of the objectives in the survey is to substantially improve overall satisfaction, the key to changing it would be to find the highest impact items. Note that there is no overlap between the two lists.

This same technique may be used to help understand which items are strongly associated with negative survey issues. In the above list with the most negative scores, note that three items in the list deal with a similar theme:

- Job assignments tend to be given based on who can do the job rather than on who needs new growth and development opportunities.
- The only way people in this organization can get ahead is to go into management.
- Once job assignments are made, people tend to get stuck in them.

It appears that the employees in this sample are very frustrated about their career and development opportunities. By creating an index of these three items and correlating them with the other survey items, you can discover which items have the most influence over career satisfaction. The items with the highest correlation are:

- There is adequate opportunity for individual growth and career development for me in this organization.
- The organization provides me with appropriate training opportunities for my professional growth.
- The management keeps its commitments to employees.
- Organization values are merely nice words. Those at the top tend to say one thing but do another.
- Management shows favoritism toward some employees and not others.

This list provides additional understanding of how to make significant improvement on these three negative items. Providing additional career and training opportunities seems obvious. But also note that the next three items deal with management's keeping its commitments and avoiding favoritism. These items are key drivers of career satisfaction.

An R&D organization was concerned about retaining its employees. As part of the employee survey, the company included the following item:

> "I rarely think about quitting my current job
> and going to a different company."

To understand what survey items impacted the intention to stay or leave, the results from the above item were correlated with all other items in the survey. The results provided a list of 16 items with reasonably high correlation. The 16 items were then factor-analyzed, a statistical technique used to cluster items into groups, resulting in three clusters. The three clusters provided a clear picture of the issues that impacted employee retention. The factor analysis provided a summary of the issues in three focused themes:

Factor 1: Relationship with Immediate Manager

- My immediate manager does a good job of celebrating team success.
- Innovative ideas are usually fully considered and explored.
- If I do my job especially well, I am confident that I will be rewarded for my effort.
- My immediate manager works effectively with people who have different backgrounds to leverage the benefits of different perspectives.
- My immediate manager learns from mistakes and changes behavior as a result of what was learned.
- My immediate manager does a good job of coaching and training me to help me improve my effectiveness.
- My immediate manager is recognized and rewarded for people development as well as for getting results.

Factor 2: Job and Company Satisfaction

- I am confident that I will be treated fairly.
- Generally, I am satisfied with this company as a place to work.
- My job and the work I do make coming to work a positive experience.
- Generally, I am satisfied with my current job.

Factor 3: Management Trust and Respect

- Respect for the individual is reflected in my management team's decisions and actions.
- My management team keeps its commitments to employees.
- Promotional opportunities go to the best-qualified candidates within my organization.
- My organization has created a working environment of trust and support.
- The management team is trusted by those within the organization.

A financial services company conducted an employee survey. The survey contained a thorough assessment of supervisory effectiveness. Eighteen items in the survey were used to evaluate the effectiveness of an individual's immediate supervisor. Results from the index (see Figure 7.16) indicated that supervisory effectiveness was quite positive overall. Examining the index in greater detail provided additional insight into the current state of supervisory effectiveness in the company.

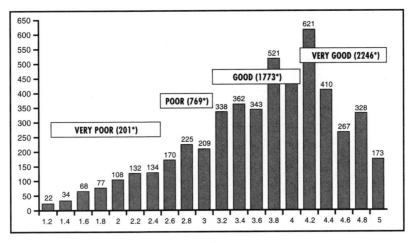

Figure 7.16: Survey results on supervisory effectiveness.

The distribution indicated that 80 percent of the employees rated their immediate supervisors as good or very good. However, 20 percent of the supervisors were rated poor or very poor. Relative to other items in the survey, the supervisory effectiveness items were not rated negatively. In fact, they were among the most positive items. But in the impact analysis the supervisory satisfaction items showed high impact on overall satisfaction. This indicated that these items had significant influence over the other survey items.

To help understand the influence of the supervisory effectiveness results, employee surveys were grouped according to how they rated their supervisors (such as very poor, poor, good, or very good). Results on the other survey items not directly associated with the supervisor were then examined. Figure 7.17 shows the percent of positive responses on the item, "This organization creates an environment where people want to go the extra mile."

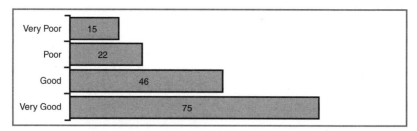

Figure 7.17: Survey results on working environment.

Note that, of the employees who rated their supervisor very poor, only 15 percent indicated that they had an environment where they wanted to "go the extra mile," while 75 percent of those with very good supervisors responded positively. Results from another item, "I'd recommend this company as a good place to work for someone like myself," showed the same trend (see Figure 7.18).

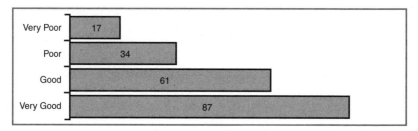

Figure 7.18: Survey results show the company is a good place to work.

This data was very helpful for this particular company for understanding the impact of poor supervisors. Employees with poor supervisors not only felt negatively about their supervisors but also about many other aspects of their work. Most of the employees with poor supervisors would not recommend the company while those with good supervisors would recommend it. It became clear to the executives that by improving the skills of these ineffective supervisors, great improvement could be made in other indices on the survey.

Impact analysis and correlation are very powerful, but the results can become very confusing. One consultant became carried away with the power of this technique and correlated each index and item with every other item and then presented it to managers, asking them to figure it out. The only thing the managers concluded was that they would never hire the consultant again. Managers gain the most benefit from an analysis that identifies items that are most likely to leverage change.

Year-to-Year Trends

Many organizations conduct surveys on an annual or semiannual basis. Keep in mind that regular surveys lead to the expectation of change or improvement. Managers begin to wonder what differences will be found from one year to another, asking questions such as, "What would a significant improvement look like?" or "How difficult is it to make a significant change in the overall results?" or "Is it possible that our results could get worse?" Figures 7.19 through 7.22 show the percent of positive responses from several different organizations from one year to another.

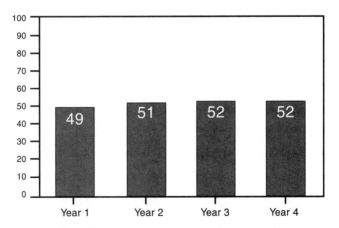

Figure 7.19: Example 1 of year-to-year comparisons of survey results.

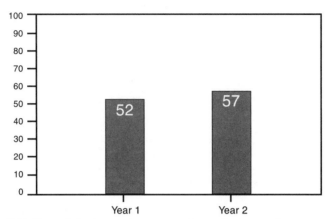

Figure 7.20: Example 2 of year-to-year comparisons of survey results.

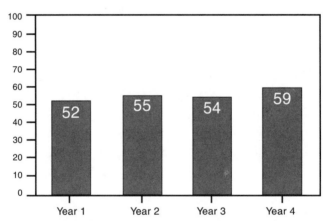

Figure 7.21: Example 3 of year-to-year comparisons of survey results.

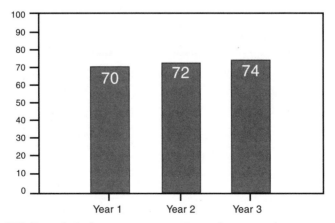

Figure 7.22: Example 4 of year-to-year comparisons of survey results.

The four examples illustrate the following conclusions:

1. Merely conducting a survey does not ensure that changes or improvements will occur. Many organizations conduct surveys yearly with little or no resulting change.

2. Results can become more negative from one year to another.

3. A five-percent improvement in the percent of positive responses on an overall index (such as on an index that is a summary of most or all the items in a survey) is substantial.

4. Not all gains are equal. Example 4 (Figure 7.22) shows results from an organization with extremely positive scores (70 percent positive in the first year). Thus, a two-percentage-point gain from year to year in this company would be substantial. In fact, simply maintaining the 70 percent positive result would require a great deal of effort.

Comment Themes

Written comments provide another valuable source of insight into survey results. The comments from surveys can provide both the specifics and the feelings behind lifeless numbers and statistics. In some cases, executives who were not compelled to action by numerical results became substantially more committed as they read the written comments.

The advantage of written comments is found in their clarity and specificity. The problem is that comments are often difficult to analyze. Typically, in analysis, each comment should be assigned a theme. Then various demographic groups or organizational levels in the survey may be analyzed using the themes. The following is a list of some of the most common positive and negative written comment themes. This analysis aggregates results from 13 different organizations in various industries.

Most Common Positive Written Comment Themes

- Liking my co-workers
- Freedom and autonomy
- Nature of the work I do
- Great company
- Customer satisfaction
- Good products/services
- Opportunities for development
- Work environment
- Pay equal to performance
- Spirit of teamwork
- Great management
- Good work/life benefits
- Flexible work schedule
- President is very effective

Most Common Negative Written Comment Themes

- Poor communication
- Need stronger management/leadership
- Better training
- Improve planning
- More empowerment
- Inefficient internal processes
- Pay is not equal to performance
- Inadequate rewards and recognition
- Inefficient computer systems
- People don't feel accountability for results
- Lack of clear goals/strategy
- Need more head count
- Lack of sufficient resources
- Poor teamwork
- Workload is too great
- Customer service is poor
- Nothing is done about poorly performing employees
- Inadequate feedback

Keys to Analyzing Employee Survey Data

Next to the design of the survey instrument, the effective analysis of results is the second most critical issue necessary for a successful survey project. Most organizations encounter two frequent problems in their analysis efforts. The first is called "analysis paralysis." Results are compared, contrasted, correlated, factor-analyzed, charted, reviewed, discussed, measured, debated, and trivialized to the point that it is no longer clear what the results mean. Intensive analysis is always recommended for any good survey effort, but analysis without interpretation is simply numbers on paper. The art of interpreting data takes a great deal of analysis, but in the end provides a simple story. The story needs to be interesting to read and have a conclusion. Effective analysis takes sophisticated analytical techniques and then draws out simple conclusions. Executives need to understand the story of the results. Sophisticated analysis can be presented in simple ways that help people at all levels of the organization understand what the data means.

The second problem with analysis efforts is called "analysis ineptitude." This occurs when data is not rigorously analyzed. Despite the wealth of descriptive reports that might indicate important trends or differences, too often conclusions are formed after only limited and cursory analysis. One company required their analysis to be summarized on no more than one page.

Although it is often valuable to be simple and to the point, such oversimplification can discourage adequate analysis of the data. Think of your survey results as a gold mine. There are huge nuggets buried deep in the mine. These nuggets cannot be found except through sufficient searching. Nobody will be interested in the many worthless tailings dug up in the process. The nuggets alone will provide the keys to creating a more successful organization.

Steps in Analysis

Start with clean data. Often in the analysis process, the data set contains errors or survey questions that should not be included. Use these steps in analysis:

1. Start the analysis with broad cuts of the data and general conclusions.

2. Break out the results by various groups to look for what is consistent and what is different.

3. Try a variety of analysis methods to look at the results in different ways and from different points of view.

4. Track down unusual or unique results. Find out when the results are and are not occurring, and why.

5. Formulate some initial conclusions.

6. Look at the written comments for verification.

7. Create a simple story outlining the results.

8. Tell the story as graphically as possible.

9. Avoid getting sidetracked by minor differences.

Remember: Ultimately, you're only searching for a few key issues that will create a fundamental change in the organization. Recommending too much action will only doom that action to failure because there will be too much to change. Formulate your final conclusions and make them simple and to the point.

CHAPTER EIGHT

Root-Cause Analysis

A *manufacturing company* decided to conduct an employee survey. The company had conducted surveys in the past, but many felt the process had raised too many expectations that were never met. In this new survey effort, the company decided to focus only on issues that were actionable and that would help the company achieve its strategic objectives. The company was currently experiencing pressure to lower its production costs while maintaining high quality.

The survey was designed and reviewed by executives to make sure that each item would be actionable. Each employee was given the opportunity to participate in the survey, and over 75 percent of them completed and returned the survey forms. The results were analyzed, showing that one of the most negative survey issues was the organization's ability to manage bureaucracy. The results are shown in Figure 8.1.

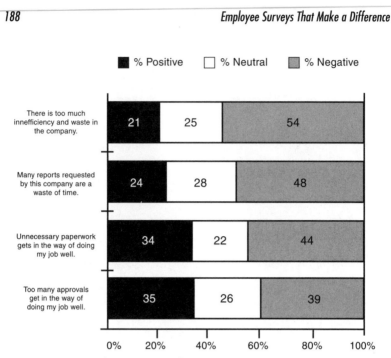

Figure 8.1: Survey results on managing bureaucracy.

After the survey, it was clear to the company's manage-ment that the bureaucracy was affecting company costs by creating tremendous inefficiency. Several managers were quick to recommend that action should be taken on this issue. A task force was created and given the specific responsibility of addressing the bureaucracy issue. The task force members met and studied the issue. They decided to identify redundant reports and processes that could be eas-ily eliminated to improve efficiency. The task force worked actively for over a year and found many duplicate reports and processes that were soon eliminated.

In the following year, a follow-up survey was conducted. This survey asked many of the same questions from the first survey. Overall, the company had shown improvement over the previous survey, and several issues showed significant change. But when the bureaucracy was analyzed, it was obvious that there had been no improvement from the employees' perspective. In fact, as the data in Figure 8.2

shows, two of the items were responded to more negatively in the follow-up survey then in the original survey.

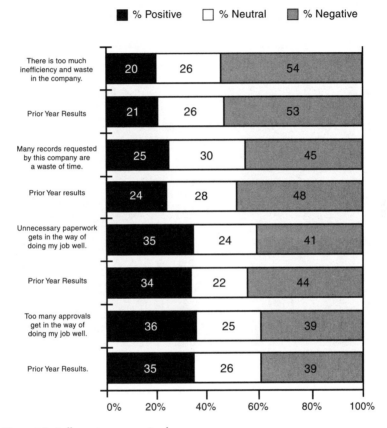

Figure 8.2: Follow-up on managing bureaucracy.

Organizational problems are complex. Often, the issue that seems most obvious is only a signal or symptom of the real problem. The fact that no significant improvement had occurred was disappointing to several of the executives and the task force. As the task force members reviewed why the employees had not perceived any substantial change, they decided that their approach to change had been incremental.

Although the team had done away with many redundant reports and processes, their approach had only focused on the leaves rather than on the roots of the problem. They began to see that, given the organization's ability to create new redundant processes, there had likely been as many new duplicate processes and reports created in the period as had been eliminated. In order to make meaningful change on this issue, the organization would have to make changes at the root of this problem, not the leaves.

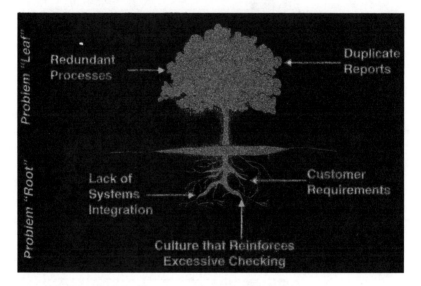

Figure 8.3: Root-cause example: excessive bureaucracy.

Root-Cause Analysis Process

Like trees, complex organizational problems have many roots. Sometimes the issues found in survey results are very straightforward and easy to resolve. Other times, they are complex and difficult to see, let alone change. Many executives have developed what I call the "Nike approach" to problem-solving: When problems arise, they ask their managers to "just fix it." As Peter Senge observes, this style of management tends to be a "quick fix" that not only doesn't address the underlying problem, but also contributes to it.[1] Although managers are often motivated and desire to generate significant improvements, complex organizational problems are often very difficult to change. Frequently, the presenting problem is not the actual problem.

Root-cause analysis is a seven-step approach that helps uncover the roots of complex organizational problems. This approach should be used in evaluating all broad organizational change efforts. If the issues are straightforward, then the process will go quickly and the solutions will be obvious. Many issues, when first presented, appear to be straightforward and easy to change.

For example, organizations frequently receive feedback that their communication could be more effective. In responding to these issues, organizations create employee newsletters, send videotaped speeches to managers, and have large group meetings to communicate the same messages to everyone at once. Sometimes this helps, but more often it is ineffective. For some organizations, the solution to a communications problem is not the frequency or volume of communications, but the accuracy (such as, "Is what management saying actually true?").

Issues that require root-cause analysis have the following characteristics:

- The issues are complex.
- The issue may not appear complex, but the solution is.
- Issues are often driven by multiple sources.
- The presenting issue may not be the actual issue.
- The issue is nested (for example: B, which is caused by C, D, and E, causes A to happen).

Most executives in organizations don't have the time or patience to unravel complex organizational problems. You might argue that it isn't even their job. Regardless of whether it is or not, my experience in presenting organizational issues to an executive team generally leads to (1) an enthusiastic speech by the group leader, (2) employees are encouraged to make significant changes on the issues presented, (3) group members nod in approval, and (4) the organization goes about its business the same as before.

If you talk to the executives one month later, they still remember the issues and are quite sure that someone in the organization is either doing something about the issues or they have a prepackaged solution that will solve everything. Executives may even remind their direct reports of the issues in subsequent meetings, and, again, the direct reports nod and say, "Right." Each is sure that *someone else* is working on the issues or that the issues have been solved.

Too often we encourage such poor problem-solving because we design processes in which survey issues are presented to the executives with no time or resources allocated to conducting root-cause analysis. A better way would be to present the results to the executives, who are then charged with deciding which issues to address first. They can then turn the issue over to a task force or steering committee for root-cause analysis and the development of an action plan. The root-cause analysis uses the following seven steps:

Step 1: Form a Task Force or Steering Committee

The process begins with the formation of a task force or steering committee to conduct the root-cause analysis.[2] The steering committee originally formed to create, administer, and analyze the survey may not have the appropriate membership to conduct root-cause analysis on specific problems. Thus, there may be one task force responsible for root-cause analysis for all issues, or there may be several smaller task forces, working with the steering committee, assigned to one issue each.

By assigning separate task forces to specific issues, it is possible to handpick task force members who have specific knowledge or experience with the issues being addressed (for example, members of the IS group or R&D may be assigned to work on issues dealing with technology improvement). The group may vary in size, depending on the issue(s) being examined. Most groups include 6 to 12 people. If more issues are to be analyzed, a larger group may be required. Do not add more people on the team as a way to manage the time commitments of team members (e.g., person A can do the first half, and person B can do the second half).

Characteristics essential for team members include:

Time. People on the team must be allowed to spend sufficient time away from their regular work assignments to accomplish the work of the team. Some people may be good potential team members, but their current schedule might not allow them any flexibility. Avoid the temptation to ask people to simply "squeeze" this into their current activities. This often creates a suboptimal process because team members are stretched too thin. Time commitments may vary depending on the issue. And, after the first few meetings, a more precise time estimate should be available. Members should be prepared to spend between 25 percent and 50 percent of their time on the project for one to two months.

Commitment. Team members must have a desire to work on this project, rather than taking it on because they feel obligated. Team members who are committed and interested in the process are more willing to spend the time and effort to make the project successful.

Broad perspective. Team members are most helpful when they have a broad perspective of organizational issues. Often teams are tempted to bring a member to the team because of a narrow technical perspective; this is not recommended. Instead, involve such specialists in the process without making them a part of the task force. Team members need broad perspective.

Executive representation. One member of the team should be an executive. When change requires tough decisions to be made, executives can help with the buy-in process.

Broad representation. The team needs to be diverse. Without diversity there may be no difference in perspective to question assumptions or raise alternative explanations to problems. Diversity here refers not only to culture, race, gender, and age, but also to a representation of the diverse jobs, locations, and personalities within an organization.

Access. Team members need access to information and other people. In order for members to be effective they will need to interview people and possibly customers. They will need to access information and will also need some analysis done.

Mission. Each team needs a clearly defined mission and commission from executives to find a solution to the issues that have been selected.

Budget. Some aspects of the team's work may require travel, research, or additional analysis. Adequate resources should be allocated to fund these activities.

Step 2: Clarify the Issue

At the kick-off of the process, the team should take time to review the survey data and clearly understand what the issue is as identified by the survey results.

• The team should review the results that were presented to the executives so that they will fully understand the findings from the survey.

• Items that define the issue specifically should be isolated and reviewed in greater detail.

• Written comments that relate to the issue should be reviewed in detail.

• A correlation analysis should be conducted where correlations exist between the issues of focus and all other issues measured in the survey. This analysis will show which issues tend to occur concurrently with the issue in focus.

• A second correlation analysis ought to be conducted comparing survey measures with other available organizational measures (measures of unit profitability, productivity, waste, sales, turnover, grievances, or customer satisfaction). The purpose of this analysis is to understand both the impact of the issue on other organizational measures and outcomes, and to better understand issues that move concurrently with the issue.

• Analysis of organizational structures (divisions, departments, and work groups) should be done to identify the best and worst performers on the issue. The purpose is to understand if the issue is consistently negative across the organization or whether there are small pockets where the issue is positive. Interviews may be conducted in the most positive and most negative groups in order to better understand the differences.

After the appropriate analyses have been conducted, the team needs to review the data to develop a thorough understanding of the results. At the conclusion of this process, an executive summary should be prepared that outlines a concise report of the conclusions of the analysis.

"Is/Is not" analysis. Another analysis that can add further clarity to an issue is the "Is/Is Not" analysis. Too often, issues are enlarged or expanded into several different issues—all packaged as the issue of focus. The "Is/Is Not" analysis helps clarify what the issue "Is" and what the issue "Is Not." Table 8.4 is an example of this analysis on the issue of collaboration.

Is	Is Not
• Lack of cooperation between groups. • Poor communication between groups where a pass-off or assistance is required. • Focus on collaboration issues that negatively impact productivity.	• Lack of cooperation within work groups. • Poor communication from executives on global issues or programs. • Focus on collaboration issues that create frustration or conflict between groups, but do not negatively impact productivity.

Figure 8.4: *Example of an Is/Is Not analysis.*

This example helps demonstrate the value of this analysis. Note that this particular issue focuses on collaboration problems between groups, not on teamwork problems within groups. The issue focuses on communication problems where pass-offs occur as part of the issue, but communications problems, in general, are not. Most important, collaboration problems between groups that cause frustration and conflict, but that do not negatively impact productivity, are not the issue of focus. Only collaboration issues that negatively impact productivity will be focused on in the root-cause analysis process.[3]

Step 3: Map Potential Root Causes

After the team has developed greater clarity on the issue, they will be ready to brainstorm a hypothetical root-cause map. This map provides the logic for the source or cause of issues and provides a weighting for each root to indicate which root has more impact. The purpose of creating the map is to help team members broaden their thinking about potential root causes. The process may be used incorrectly if team members lock on to this logic without verification.

The map provides hypotheses that need to be tested, not well-founded conclusions.

Base root model. The starting point for the root-cause map is a set of characteristics of organizations that act as root bases. Each of the bases represents a potential cause at a high level of abstraction. It is not likely that all of the bases will have causes associated with them. However, the model does act as a brainstorming tool to help understand potential causes of problems.

Equipment or technology. Problems in this root are based on unreliable or inadequate equipment or technology. Technology is often viewed as an easy solution to many informational or technical problems. Typically, improved equipment or technology does not solve any problems in and of themselves. Instead, new technology and equipment are only as effective as the systems and processes that support them.

One company survey raised the issue of poor quality. As the various root causes were examined, one team member commented, "The people charged with reviewing the designs have very small monitors. They can see only a portion of the design at any one time, so they have to scroll back and forth. It's no surprise to me that they make a few mistakes. In fact, I'm surprised they haven't made more errors."

Company strategy. The source for many problems lies in unclear or inadequate strategies. Functions may also have confusing strategies that do not relate to the overall company strategy. Although most companies have a strategy, the strategy often fails to empower employees in a way that guides and directs their work. A strategic direction, such as producing a high return for shareholders, does not provide any direction to employees as to how they will accomplish that goal. Problems rooted in strategy sometimes reinforce one behavior or approach when another is needed, while other times the current strategy lacks the clarity required to drive performance.

Organizational structure. An organizational chart formally describes a company's structure. It is often said that organization structures were created to solve problems that no longer exist. That is why, many times, organizational structures are not as useful as they could be in helping to facilitate strategic objectives. These structures tend to develop a "built-in resource and emotional investment in the continuance of the established design."[4] Organizational structures can be useful when they are used to reinforce the differences in the way people think and behave. Strong functional organizations tend to reinforce functional thinking, while cross-functional structures reinforce integrative thinking across several different functions. Problems rooted in structure typically exist when the structure reinforces behaviors or attitudes that either run counter to the issue being addressed, or to other issues.

Systems or processes. Systems are the glue that keeps organizations functioning. But they also reinforce behaviors and attitudes in people. In a reward system that compensates employees for individual performance it is difficult to get people to work in teams and to collaborate. Processes designed to ensure quality do not encourage efficiency unless, of course, improved quality also increases efficiency. A common root-cause of many problems is found in the systems and processes of the organization that reinforce opposing opinions and attitudes. Systems and processes are also effective ways to cause changes in an organization. By taking an informal process and designing a system to measure desired outcomes, reward appropriate behavior, and monitor performance, companies can produce profound change.

Company culture or values. The culture of an organization is a set of commonly held beliefs and values. Many of these values are not formally recognized or written down, but they are clearly taught. New employees are schooled in the culture and taught the company's values. As a result, the cultures created over time are not always intended. Different cultures can arise among different business units, frustrating the accomplishment of a company strategy.[5]

For example, an adversarial relationship may exist between the labor union and management. The norms teach management that the union is simply motivated to get more entitlements for its members. Likewise, union members are taught that management tries to take advantage of union members, and that management doesn't care about the union's needs and concerns.

Problems frequently arise when the culture reinforces opposing behaviors or attitudes. Sometimes a culture dictates what is possible within an organization. Many organizations benchmark themselves against others and then try to recreate another organization's culture within their own. Completely changing a culture takes an enormous amount of time, effort, and money.

People. Having the right people is a huge strength for any organization. We revere that special individual who is always able to accomplish the impossible. Many organizations acknowledge this in their value statements, saying, "Employees are our most valuable asset." But this statement often frustrates employees who don't see the actions of executives as consistent with that value. Root causes that have to do with people typically relate to the poor fit between jobs and people. This may occur when the wrong people are promoted or when there is a lack of clarity about hiring requirements.

Individual competence. People have great capacity to learn new skills and master difficult competencies. Successful organizations are created when people learn new skills required for changing environments. Although people with new skills are often hired from outside the organization, they sometimes lack knowledge of the organization itself. An organization's ability to help employees learn new skills is a critical factor for success. Root-cause problems occur here when the source of the problem comes from the lack of skills in employees. The difference between the "individual competence" root and the "people" root is that people have the capacity to learn, possess a willingness to adapt, and can help save time and money on teaching.

Management style. Management style refers to the approach and the authority people use to accomplish company objectives. Styles may range from a very autocratic style, to a very involved, results-driven style, to a strong technical orientation. There is not necessarily a "best" style, but different styles produce different outcomes. At times, the predominant management style may conflict with desired outcomes. Root causes in this area come when the management style produces undesirable side effects. Individual managers may have differing styles, but each company has a style that predominates.

Customers. Root causes that have their source in customers come from either poor understanding of customer needs or from unsuccessful attempts to satisfy the needs of the wrong customers. Customer needs change over time. Most organizations have difficulty staying current with the needs and desires of customers. Competitors constantly approach customers with unique approaches that differentiate their products or services. This encourages customers to raise the bar in terms of their expectations: quality, service, and time lines.

Many companies attempt to focus 80 percent of their attention on 20 percent of their customers. But customers with requirements outside of the company's core competency can create significant problems. When addressing root causes relating to customers, make sure you do not blame the customers for your problems. Much like the librarian who blames all the complexities of running a library on "those people who check out books," organizations must clearly understand what customers want and which customers they want to serve, and then design strategies, systems, and processes to achieve superior performance.

Competitors. Occasionally companies become confused about what is happening in the competitive environment. They seem to produce the same or similar products, with the same quality, and provide them to the same customers, but they keep losing orders to their competitors. An internal search for problems reveals nothing.

When competitors are the root-cause, the problem is that the competitors have changed the external environment. The company has very little knowledge about what the competitors are doing and how their company is distinct from the competition. But it is vital that companies consciously differentiate themselves from the competition if they want to obtain or maintain a competitive advantage.[6] Tracking root causes back to competitors provides the logic for what else may need to change internally in order for change in the marketplace to occur.

What Causes "Too Much Bureaucracy"?

The following is an example of a brainstorming session on the problem described in the beginning of this chapter. Base roots (sets of organizational characteristics) are bolded with a description of the base root following. Each base root also provides weights. The total weight equals 100.

Equipment or technology (Weight 15).
- Too many paper processes. Shared databases and information systems could eliminate some bureaucracy.

Company Strategy
Organizational structure (Weight 10).

- A strong functional organization. We are efficient within functions, but create information needs in checking across functional boundaries.
- Top-down decision-making requires a great deal of information at higher levels of the organization.

Systems or processes (Weight 10).
- Most organizations have free reign to request information from any other group on an as-needed basis.

Company culture or values (Weight 20).
- Tendency to check on, and get a sign off for, everything. Example: expense reports need to be signed off by three layers of management.
- Lack of trust in lower-level managers; hence the need to check, check, check.
- Executives who don't check are viewed as not doing their job.

People/Individual Competence

Management style (Weight 5).
- A cover-your-own-rear-end attitude translates into people needing every detail for all work groups under their control.

Customers (Weight 40).
- Customer requirements call for detailed reports on every aspect of our product.

In this example, note that the map is not exceptionally complex, but it does identify the base roots that need to be investigated. Also, note that the customer base got the highest weight. The customers required an exceptional amount of documentation, which created significant bureaucracy. This assumption stimulated many other questions, such as:

- If these are all requirements from the customer, then is there little we can do to change?

- Can we negotiate with our customers on this documentation?
- Can we use information systems to automatically collect the data?
- Who in the customer's organization requires this documentation?

On the other hand, putting 40 points on this issue may be an easy way for the team to blame the bureaucracy on their customer. When validated, the team may find that, in actuality, the customer requirements are not extraordinary. In fact, this team later found that the customers asked for a little, but the company expanded on the original request.

The next step in the process is to take this initial map and research the most significant base causes to uncover the accuracy of the model and the respective weights of the parts. The need to validate the model soon becomes obvious.

Step 4: Validate the Issues

After the initial map is created, the team then tries to validate the model. Rather than validating every root of the model, the team should select three or four major roots for thorough validation. The criteria for which roots should be validated are based on (1) the weights assigned to each root, and (2) the ease of change. After the roots have been selected, the next task is to create a plan to validate the three or four roots. The process of validation will differ, depending on the specifics of each root-cause.

The validation process starts by dividing the team into subteams and then assigning each subteam a particular analysis. This helps the process move faster and allows fewer people to go into greater depth, rather than having everyone try to analyze each issue. Dividing into subteams also allows different perspectives to form as people focus in on their own unique analysis. Each team then proceeds with its data-gathering chores. Some teams may require additional resources to accomplish their task. Any one of several tools may be used in the validation process:

Interviews. Probably the most common process is interviewing. The interviewing is simple: Ask people what they think. Keep in mind that the process tells you what people *believe* to be true, rather than what is actually true. For this reason, when interviewing you should take careful consideration with those who may not initially understand your assumptions. Interviews can validate conventional wisdom that is well-known and communicated around the company.

Don't be surprised, in the interviewing process, when people don't seem to "see the forest for the trees." People are usually accurate about what they experience, but they do not always understand why things occur. Therefore, the interviews should focus primarily on what people experience, how frequently they experience it, and what impact the experience has on them. Asking them to speculate about why they are having such experiences may be interesting, but it will not necessarily be valid. Many will tend to blame other people for their problems rather than the systems, process, or equipment. ("This would work fine if only those people knew how to do it right!")[7] Interviews are always more effective when conducted by a few people, rather than by a whole committee.

Outcome analysis. This process attempts to gather hard data on outcomes. Root processes are loosely associated with outcomes. How often does an outcome occur? When does it occur? When does it not occur? What occurs prior to the outcome? What occurs after the outcome? Often, it can be helpful to measure the costs, the waste, or the profits of particular outcomes. Customers can also provide historical data on volume, activity, profits, and so forth.

Process analysis. Most processes are well-known in organizations but not well-understood. And, because the processes become fragmented between departments, people understand only their own part of the process, not the parts that others handle. A process map simply maps out processes in detail. Once the processes are mapped, it becomes easy to see how a process could be made more efficient.

Best-practice comparison. This is a useful tool to help the team understand how other groups or companies have solved similar problems. In some companies, internal groups have managed to become significantly more effective on an issue than other groups in the company. In addition, some companies are very effective at particular skills. One company, which sold countertops and sinks, wanted to improve their speed of delivery to customers. They benchmarked themselves against a company that changed the oil in cars in 15 minutes or less. Benchmark comparisons such as these don't need to be in the same industry. Frequently, the critical issues you are benchmarking have little to do with the industry.

Similar-industry analysis. When organizations are going through a major change, one helpful practice is to study a similar industry that has gone through a similar change. One organization dealing with the applications of its new equipment studied the banking industry to understand which bank most successfully used automated teller machines.

Future analysis. Using analytical tools that extrapolate future trends from current data, this analysis provides a glimpse into the future. By examining what has happened in similar industries and then extrapolating from current data, these predictions are sometimes very accurate. The analysis is most useful when trying to prepare for an uncertain future. At times, issues will arise in an organization and the consensus will be that the company is not serious enough to change right then. A future analysis can help the organization anticipate a scenario in the future when there would be a greater need for skills in a particular area.

Moving ahead. The team needs to gather together weekly for progress reports. Each subteam keeps up with the pace and makes meaningful work. Since the subteams can get off-target in these analyses, it is important to track their progress regularly. As the teams conclude their analysis, they should prepare reports that summarize their analysis and recommendations. The reports should provide sufficient detail to back up conclusions and recommendations. After all the teams have prepared their reports, the whole team joins together to share their conclusions and decide on the implications of the various analyses.

Step 5: The Subteam Report

At the conclusion of the validation process the team prepares an overall report with general conclusions. Sometimes the different analysis conducted by subteams all lead to the same conclusion. Other times the analysis may lead to two or more different conclusions. When this occurs, teams may want to participate in an advocacy process to decide on their strategic direction.

Randy Stott, Norm Smallwood and Jon Younger of Novations Group, Inc., used such a process to help organizations decide on their strategies. In the advocacy process, members of the subteams are asked to assume that theirs is the correct conclusion and that the goal is to prove all other subteams wrong. The process allocates time for each subteam to prepare detailed analysis, conclusions, and defenses. Rather than assigning people who believe, up front, any of the conclusions being advocated, subteam members should be assigned randomly. The subteams then make their presentations with the goal of persuading all other subteams to accept their issue. The advocacy process is very useful in helping the whole team decide upon a strategy that best fits the needs of the organization.[8]

The group then prepares a final report and updates the root-cause map to fit their conclusions before it moves on to the next step: action planning. In many cases, the team should review their report with executives at this point, prior to action planning. If there is concern over management's willingness to accept the conclusions of the analysis, then action plans will be of little value without the input of executives. Some groups, after preparing their conclusions, may still lack the validation necessary to convince others in the organization to take action. At this point the team may go back and perform additional validation work to verify their conclusions.

Step 6: Plan for Change

Once the team has decided on the cause, they must now focus on what needs to change. The team must examine various questions, such as: Which things are easy to change, and which will be difficult? Which issues are internally or externally controlled? These questions and the change processes outlined in Chapter 9 will help. The most critical issue at this point is determining which few changes will have the greatest impact on the overall issue. Apply the 80/20 rule, trying to get 80 percent or more of the desired changes from just a few actions. Such a concentrated focus will greatly benefit the company because organizations can focus only limited energy or resources on multiple initiatives.

Once the team has reached a consensus on the approach, they must present their report to executive management. An important element of the change plan is who will be responsible for the recommendations and for carrying out the plan. The task force will not usually execute the recommendations for change, but any good action plan will assign this responsibility to a specific person.

Do not assign responsibilities to the executives without their agreement. The task force needs to create a very clear and persuasive presentation that will convince executives and employees at all levels of both the logic of the root-cause and the importance of the actions that will be required to make the changes work. The logic is critical because without the logic it will be difficult for people to associate the change with the issues identified in the survey.

A large organization had just completed its first organizational climate survey. The results were presented to top managers and then to all other managers and supervisors. The results showed a strong positive climate but several negative issues. One of the most negative issues was collaboration. Comments included:

- "Many groups in the company are competing against each other, detrimentally, for equipment, people, money, or recognition."
- "There is lot of duplication of effort because work groups don't collaborate."
- "Company resources and money are wasted because work groups don't work together."

The issue was accepted as a universal problem for the company. A task force was assigned to conduct a root-cause analysis on the issues. The analysis found several root causes, but the primary root centered around a reward system that rewarded groups for not sharing resources, causing them to compete with each other. Although it was clear throughout the organization that poor collaboration was a problem, people in every work group were still pleased with the reward system and did not want to give it up. In this case, the logic for the change was critical so everyone would understand the relationship between the reward system and the poor collaboration it instigated.

Making the plan specific. To make a plan for change effective it must be specific, spelling out the change process and identifying the people responsible for executing particular objectives. The task force needs to be careful at this point: The goal is to create a total plan for change without overwhelming the executives. The team may choose to present the plan piece-by-piece so the executives can "eat the elephant one bite at a time."

Often, the final conclusions may threaten some groups or individuals. But, if the logic is well accepted, it can then be followed by the change plan; then, individuals will not be arguing against the logic of the root-cause when the change plan seems to threaten their position or security. If people can first agree on the logic of the root-cause, then the change plan will be a foregone conclusion.

But the logic, however compelling, will be of no value without a detailed plan for change. If the change plan has any perceived negative implications in the organization, the team may find itself facing enormous political forces at work to keep from moving the change plan forward. The process for presenting the survey results needs to be well-established up front so as to not be put on the shelf and forgotten about.

Presenting the root-cause logic in one step, and the plan for change in a second step, allows people in the company to add additional value and insight to the root-cause logic. These modifications may change the action required.

Step 7: Present the Root-Cause Analysis and Recommendations

It is critical that appropriate time and resources are allocated to ensure that the team is adequately prepared for its presentation. The team must consider the best way to present the information in a clear and persuasive manner.

Short and to the point. Long and complex presentations are rarely persuasive. Instead, they are usually quite boring. The team must determine what it needs to say and then present their ideas in a clear, concise, and candid way. Although the report is usually made in presentation format, the presentation may be accompanied by a written document with additional details. The presentation should be compelling. Pictures and charts can communicate better than words, and models are usually better than lists.

Energetic speakers. The team also must decide who will present the data. Sometimes team members can share amongst themselves the task of making the presentation, which can make a longer or more detailed presentation more interesting. Also, if executives see employees who may not have had a vested interest in a particular point of view presenting the data, it may help them to agree. On the other hand, shared presentations are frequently difficult to control and some team members can be more persuasive than others. The team must make a high-quality presentation rather than a popular decision in this matter.

Compelling data. If, when going into the presentation, the data is not compelling, gather more data or adjust your conclusions. Executives love to shoot holes in poor logic, and, when root-cause reports lack the integrity to stand up under difficult questions, they never succeed. On the other hand, it does not take enormous amounts of compelling data to convince both executives and employees to take action. In fact, many executives become impatient with too many numbers.[9]

Gather buy-in up front. As we have discussed, some of the root causes the team uncovers may be entrenched in political issues that have been ignored in the organization for years. Often, the root-cause process forces the organization to pull skeletons out of the closet. In effect, these issues have been well-known, but conveniently avoided for too long. Team members can now become invigorated in the process. They may feel compelled to single-handedly take on any issue. But, although this courage is commendable, it is wise to garner support for some of the issues right off the bat. Teams must be careful that they do not break rules or violate confidences in this process; however, getting support for a difficult issue early is often critical in successfully making changes.

Reasonable actions. In the root-cause analysis process, some teams become idealistic and start to lay out extraordinary objectives. But, while they may be fun to speculate about and interesting to consider, these objectives must be discarded. Teams ought to recommend reasonable actions that lead to results in the long term while allowing people to get used to the change in the short term. In the meantime, plans must to be made with both short-term and long-term goals in mind.

Link plans to strategic objectives. Probably the most significant point, the one that will do more to compel the organization to action more than any other, is the link between the action plan and the company's strategic objectives. If people do things because they are "good" or "right," they tend to lose energy and commitment over time. Doing things because they ultimately will lead to a more competitive organization—one that will remain in business and grow—is the secret to ensuring both consistency and effort from both executives and employees. Here again, the logic is essential. We need to change "A" because it has a significant impact on "B," which will be critical in helping us achieve our strategic objectives.

Rollout throughout the organization. Although it is critical to get executive buy-in, it is also essential to get buy-in from employees throughout the organization. Executives at the top may be able to act on many issues, but it will soon be essential for employees to execute the actions without the executive driving the change. The team needs to plan how to communicate actions throughout the organization, especially when employee action will be necessary for changes to occur. An issue such as expanding the span of control and driving decision-making to lower levels needs both executive commitment and employee commitment for change to occur.

Root-Cause Analysis Works Best When . . .

People are creative. There is a tendency to put up with problems in organizations when there is no apparent solution. Consequently, people will focus more of their attention on coping with, or finding ways to work around the problem than on doing away with what causes it. Root-cause teams, to be effective, must be creative and imaginative. The creativity used at the start of the process to find the root causes must also be used at the end to make changes.

If the team considers issues only from the same perspective that has always been considered, little progress will be made. However, if the team will think outside the typical box and consider solutions not always considered, then greater progress can be made. If it were easy to solve the problems addressed by root-cause analysis, then the problems likely would have been solved already. The easy issues were already addressed. It's the issues that linger in organizations that require extraordinary creativity to solve.

All assumptions are questioned. In most organizations there is an unwritten set of rules about what is all right to consider and what remains outside the understood boundary. In terms of this analysis, things never work well with too many boundaries; they keep the team in their box, reward the status quo, and reinforce political issues that have been insulated in the past. Although some actions may not be taken outside a particular boundary, the team should be encouraged to consider every possible solution.

Team members have a broad perspective. Breadth is brought to the team by depth of experience, both within and outside the company. Although some team members may not be as experienced as others, each must be flexible and willing to consider different perspectives.

The process is recursive. A recursive process is one that builds on and reinforces itself. Using an autocratic approach to get executives to accept being more participatory, or convincing people in the organization to be more data driven on decisions while having very little data in the presentation, are examples of nonrecursive processes. Although this may sound quite simple, it is surprising to see how often groups find themselves being nonrecursive.

A root-cause analysis task force found that one of the major forces which reduced the company's speed was the need for consensus on every decision. Any decision, no matter how inconsequential, had to be reviewed up and down the organization, which had practically been paralyzing the company. After the root-cause analysis had been completed and the report prepared, the team discussed how to present the report.

The immediate plan called for them to run the report by each senior manager to get a commitment, then by the supervisors, and so on down the line. But, after discussing the plan, one task force member asked, "Isn't this what we are trying to stop?" The other team members appeared surprised, but then agreed with a resounding "yes." They finally decided to present their plan in the next executive committee meeting, and to note the difference between how they had originally decided to roll out the plan and how they changed that plan. The improvement in company speed was significant.

The company takes an external perspective. Organizations often generate extraordinary boundaries that create insular thinking and restrict learning from the outside. For a 12-month period, one software company bet that the market would go in a particular direction and refused to recognize a series of clear signals to the contrary. It should be obvious that a team cannot have an external perspective if the team focuses only on internal interviews and data. Competitive comparisons, plus the best practices and benchmarking studies, are helpful in expanding the company's external perspective.

Executives take an employee perspective. Executives in organizations are also insular at times. They inadvertently create boundaries to communication from employees at various levels of the organization. A team that relies exclusively on the executive perspective usually ends up with a distorted view.

Everyone keeps an open mind. People naturally dislike staying in an undecided or confused state. People will move quickly to formulate an opinion and then establish the logic to support it. In today's fast-paced business environment, executives feel pressured to make decisions quickly and to move forward fast. This speed is not problematic as long as people do not focus solely on their decisions, thereby ignoring information that might be different. Teams that stay open and encourage members not to lock on to one solution too quickly are always more effective in this process.

The Root of Success

Most of the easy problems have already been solved, not only by your company but by most of your competitors. Difficult problems, the ones that are not straightforward, are easy for organizations to ignore. Consider the tremendous advantage for the companies that can find these difficult solutions before others do. Companies that can solve only the simple problems are simply maintaining parity with each other. Companies that can find ways to overcome complex problems will have a competitive advantage over others.

Root-cause analysis is a fairly involved process. If your issues are simple and straightforward, then this process will not be necessary. However, it is often difficult to tell. Some issues appear straightforward, but in reality they may be very complex. After 20 years of analyzing feedback survey data, I am convinced that this process is necessary for companies to create change on many issues. Building this process up front as a standard part of the process is important. Energy is created by administering the survey and examining the results. It is easy to feel that the process is finished as soon as the data comes back; but that's where all the fun begins.

Notes to Chapter Eight

1. Peter Senge, *The Fifth Discipline*. New York: Doubleday Currency, 1990, 106-7.

2. Allen I. Kraut, "Organizational Research on Work and Family Issues" in Sheldon Zedeck, ed., *Work, Families, and Organizations*, San Francisco: Jossey-Bass, 1992, 208-35.

3. For a more detailed case study of the "Is/Is Not" analysis framework, see Perrin Stryker, "How to Analyze That Problem," *Harvard Business Review* 43 (July-August, 1965), 4:99.

4. Richard Hammermesh, ed, *Strategic Management*, New York: Wiley & Sons, 1983, 56-57.

5. Michael Porter, *Competitive Advantage*, New York: The Free Press, 1985, 390.

6. Ibid, 14.

7. Senge, *The Fifth Discipline*, 40.

8. Lee Tom Perry, Randall G. Stott, and W. Norman Smallwood, *Real-Time Strategy: Improvising Team-Based Planning for a Fast-Changing World*, New York: Wiley & Sons, 1993, 56.

9. Kraut and Kraut, *Organizational Surveys*, 199.

CHAPTER NINE

Creating Change
in Organizations

Creating change in organizations is difficult. Both executives and employees resist unintended or chaotic changes. Leaders work hard to create stable systems, processes, and employees because consistency, order, and predictability are needed in organizations. Both employees and leaders count on things being the same way tomorrow as they were today. In many ways, most changes seem unneeded since, apparently, we want to create organizations that don't change.

On the other hand, organizations face a world that is quickly changing. To survive, an organization must adapt. Organizations that are not able to make necessary adjustments will no longer exist in the future. Any organization with an ability to change quickly and efficiently in desired ways will have a substantial competitive advantage.

Change efforts are often difficult for organizations. Employees do not always cooperate. Previous changes once sold as benefits to employees often turned out to be benefits only for a few, while the rest were left skeptical and cynical, or "downsized." Change, by its very nature, creates the possibility of losing something. It also creates the possibility of winning something. The change process is usually unsure, unstable, and comes associated with some risk. Many employees would rather be secure with what they have than risk losing something. Change is inevitably messy. The process places people in unique situations where they don't know exactly what to do. Often, change requires people to perform new jobs requiring different skills. Typically, the change process brings confusion, and people generally don't like confusion.

As managers and employees begin the process of change, they sometimes believe anything is possible. "If other organizations have done this, why can't we?" And, although many organizations have gone through incredible changes, some organizations can handle the stress, but others can't. Something my father used to say captures what I'm referring to: "You can't make a silk purse out of a sow's ear." He would use that quote whenever I would attempt crazy things like trying to impress girls with our family car. The car was definitely a "sow's ear," and all my girlfriends knew it.

Organizations, like people, develop differently. They have different skills, personalities, attitudes, and abilities. An individual may desire to become a great athlete. Hard work, determination, and practice all contribute to improving one's performance, but being great is more often a function of all the above, combined with genetics. Physical size, coordination, mental ability, and other inherent traits usually make the final difference. In the same way, many organizations are limited by their genetic make-up. A dramatic change for one organization might be quite simple and only take a few months. But, for another organization it might take years, and even then it may be done only moderately well.

A variety of skills and processes can facilitate organizational change. However, the skills and processes that best facilitate change are not the same for all organizations. An organization's history and experience will help determine which skills and processes will be most useful in a successful change effort.

In this chapter I present a variety of approaches that can help organizations facilitate change. Often, to successfully implement changes, several of these approaches may have to be used. These processes and skills can be thought of as levers, and the more levers an organization employs, the more likely it will be able to succeed in its change initiatives.

1. Finding the Real Problem

A large organization had just completed its first organizational climate survey. The results were presented to the company's top managers first, and then to all other managers and supervisors. The results showed a strong positive climate, as well as several negative issues. One of the most negative issues from the data was "collaboration." Items such as the following were responded to negatively:

- "Many groups are competing against each other for equipment, people, money, or recognition to the detriment of the company."
- "Because work groups are not collaborating, the result is duplicated effort."
- "Company resources are wasted because work groups don't work together."

The feedback was generally accepted as true for the whole company. At a meeting in which the survey results were shared with all managers in the company, the president stood up and made an impassioned plea for the managers to make improvements and changes in collaboration. It felt like something positive was going to happen. But, after 18 months had passed, another survey showed that collaboration actually had become more negative than it had been. Once again, the president stood and appealed to the managers to improve. This time, he seemed even more impassioned, more focused. The managers felt terrible. They felt they had let their president down. They wanted to change and thought they could do better this time. They left the meeting again committing to do all they could to personally solve this problem. But again, after 18 months, collaboration was still a problem for the company.

The following represents a typical top-management feedback meeting:

- Present survey results.
- Top management agrees on the most important issues to change.
- Everyone agrees and becomes enthusiastic about making some change.
- Group leaders say, "I am personally committed to changing this issue, and I hope everyone here is just as committed."
- No one says they're not committed.
- Group leaders say, "Well then, let's do it! What's the next agenda item?"

Most executives don't have the patience to unravel complex organizational problems. You might argue that it isn't even their job to do so. Whether it is or isn't their job, it seems that whenever organizational feedback is presented to executives, the president or division leader typically follows with an enthusiastic speech. The leader encourages people to make significant changes based on the feedback. Group members then nod in approval, and the organization goes forth with its business.

If you talk to executives one month after this event, they still remember the feedback and the speech and are quite sure someone in the company is doing something about it. They may even remind their direct reports, and the direct reports nod and say, "Right." Each is sure that someone else is working on the problem. Many of them, in turn, share the reminder with their own direct reports, who likewise agree to work on the issue. As obvious as it seems from this apparent satire, the reason organizations don't solve their problems is because they never actually work on the problem.

The best approach for making changes on issues raised by employee surveys is to include a root-cause analysis in the survey process. As before, top executives confirm the top survey issues, but, before they give their speech, they should indicate the next step is to assign a separate group to prepare a root-cause analysis and generate action plans for the executive team's approval. Chapter 8 explains root-cause analysis and how it works.

2. Making Change a Priority

Organizational erosion. Change initiatives in organizations can be compared to rocks. These rocks experience organizational erosion. Organizational erosion is much quicker than natural erosion. For example, a person could generate a very large change-initiative rock, and within a month the rock would be half that size. Within three months the rock would be a mere pebble and hardly noticeable among all the other pebbles in the organization. You can't stop this erosion; you can only increase the size of the rocks. For change-initiative rocks to survive, you must generate huge rocks. So, the first question to ask is, "Is this change really that important?" In other words, can you justify making this change initiative huge. If the rock is only large- or medium-sized, it probably will not survive unless it can be implemented in a few short months. Change-initiative rocks that are large and never get fully eroded (or implemented) create significant distractions to the organization. They form obstacles and leave little room for other change-initiative rocks. Organizations are better off not being disrupted with change initiatives that are never implemented.

Organizations have an endless supply of activities: getting work done, training employees, maintaining and improving systems and processes, meeting customer expectations, and, of course, conducting meetings, meetings, and more meetings. When it comes to change initiatives, organizations must ask, "Can this initiative compete with all the other events and activities going on in the organization?" It seems each organization is engaged in a football game that ends only when the organization is out of business. You can call time out, but only a few times. You must get the attention of the players during those timeouts, help them improve the way they are executing. They need a new vision, a plan, a reason to change, and the motivation to do so. Organizations cannot stop to implement changes; they must change while they continue to execute.

Once you determine that a particular change initiative can hold its own with all the other activities and initiatives going on in the organization, you then need to build the case for change in the organization. The process of building a case involves the following steps:

Preparing the case for change. Just as lawyers prepare cases before they go to court, you must prepare your case for change. The following questions need persuasive arguments:

- Why does the organization need to change?
- What will happen if it doesn't change?
- What will the organization look like after the change is completed?
- Who will be affected by the change?
- How will the company go about changing?
- Who in the organization needs to be committed to this change for it to succeed?

Communicating the case for change. After preparing your case for change, the next step is to communicate the change to those who need to know. Typically, the communication process needs the following elements:

- Build support with key stakeholders.
- Occur more than once.

- Use several different mediums, such as speeches, articles in company newsletters, e-mail messages, and training programs.
- Repeat the message to stakeholders and others involved in making the change.
- Deliver a consistent message.
- Remain focused.

3. Building Support

Organizational change rarely occurs on one person's effort alone. Any change that requires cooperation from others absolutely requires support from the people who will be cooperating. Building a broad support base for organizational change is usually more difficult than it seems. I frequently see managers talk to their direct reports about change efforts. The direct reports typically express interest, excitement, and personal commitment when the managers describe the change to be made. The managers then believe the change should be fairly simple and straightforward. However, when it comes time for individuals in the group to change, they often resist changing. Most direct reports have learned the art of acting interested and committed. Also, even when direct reports are genuinely interested and committed, they often lose momentum when they realize the extent to which the change will affect them personally.

Most people underestimate the difficulty of building support. They make bold announcements before others have heard anything about the change. They expect others to be as excited and committed to the change as they, themselves, are. Managers typically assume that just because they think something is a good idea, others will naturally agree. For this reason, such a bold beginning to a difficult change process often ends in failure. Before announcing any change, managers should build a broad support base for the change, including input from stakeholders at various organizational levels.

The more support that can be lined up prior to announcing a new change initiative, the higher the probability will be that a significant change can be successfully implemented.

Gaining support for a change effort can be approached in many different ways. For example, the way you came to be committed to a change effort may not be a way that is as effective for others. People differ in how they become committed. Understanding the different ways people are motivated, and then applying the right motivation to the right people, will improve your ability to gain commitment.

4. Building Commitment

You can build support and commitment using proven tools.

Honesty and sincerity. The most universal tool for gaining support is honesty and sincerity. If people believe and trust you, they will more likely believe in and trust your change efforts. Business people are tempted almost daily to bend the facts or not to disclose all the information in a straightforward manner. Although there sometimes may be short-term reasons to use manipulative strategies, people will find out the truth in the long run and will then be much more cautious about trusting you.

Logic. Many people can be motivated to change through logical arguments. Laying out a clear picture of current reality versus the future state of things, illustrating the facts, and showing clear examples often leads to getting many people on board for the proposed change process. A good theory that can be proven is often a very useful tool. Using logic and rational arguments is probably the most common approach for gaining commitment from others. But this strategy does not work for everyone. Good logic, a well-reasoned theory, and rational arguments need to be used in addition to other tools for fostering commitment.

Friendship and loyalty. Friendship and loyalty can be used to build support in two ways: First, your friends are more likely to listen to you and trust what you say. Also, they generally are more open to your logic; second, you can sometimes ask friends to cooperate even though they have reservations. I like to look at this tool as a kind of checking account for personal favors. Through your associations with that person, you build up a line of credit based on mutual integrity and loyalty, and now you are making a withdrawal of some of that credit. Keep in mind that people tend to keep good track of the balance, and as it gets close to zero they become less willing to let you make withdrawals.

Bottom-line financial impact. It's easy for employees to forget that all organizations must deliver results, stay within budgets, and generate a reasonable profit. Some change efforts are rolled out without any apparent connection to the bottom line. Making a clear connection between proposed change efforts and their impact on the bottom line often helps people build commitment and support. Other times, employees need to be clear about the financial consequences of not implementing changes. Creating a realistic picture of a negative financial downside because change initiatives are ignored can also help generate commitment.

Reward/What's in it for me? Punishment and rewards are two effective methods of changing behavior. Having clear cause-effect relationships for specific performance standards and outcomes can have dramatic impact on support. People may argue your logic or the reality of the bottom line, but when you reward desired outcomes many people become committed. Keep in mind that there are many different rewards besides money. Some people want job security more than money; others want freedom to work without close supervision, and still others want promotions or opportunities for challenging work.

Desire to win. Good coaches help prepare their teams for big games. They help teams understand the strengths and weaknesses of the competition and then practice hard to defend themselves. Although sports analogies are frequently overused, helping people become enthusiastic about their work stimulates higher performance. Conflicts with competitors can serve to unite people who previously had fought only against each other in the company. Unions and management, research and manufacturing, or sales and production can become committed and united against a common foe.

The support test. A good test for whether you have enough support is to sit back and see how others in the organization push an initiative forward. If, when you back off, the initiative quickly loses momentum, you have not created enough support. When you have created sufficient support you will notice that others in the organization begin to drive the changes harder and more consistently than you. Also, if others become highly supportive, change initiatives typically evolve from their original concepts.

5. Keeping a Clear Vision

When I was 12 years old, I had a job working for my uncle on his farm. One Saturday, early in the spring, my uncle asked me to come with him in the truck to his grain field. He had been plowing the field but had another commitment and was going to teach me to plow. Sitting at one end of the field was a huge Caterpillar tractor. Actually, the tractor wasn't that large, but at age twelve I couldn't think of anything more fun than driving a Caterpillar.

To teach me, my uncle drove as I sat on the fender and he explained the levers and buttons. We then plowed up one row and down another. He asked if I could do it, and I replied, "No problem." He stepped down from the

Caterpillar and let me take the controls. He stood by and told me to try the next row on my own. I pulled down on the throttle, the diesel engine revved, and I felt the power as I let up on the clutch. I was totally focused on staying right on the edge of the previous furrow. I looked down by the front track of the Caterpillar and made occasional adjustments to make sure I stayed the appropriate distance from the plowed ground.

When I finished the row, my uncle stopped me and had me step off the tractor to look at my furrow. His furrow was a perfectly straight line all the way down the row, but mine was a wavy line. I had made many corrections to stay the appropriate distance from the plowed ground. My uncle congratulated me on doing a pretty good job, but then he said I needed to make one change: "Don't look down at the ground right in front of the Caterpillar; instead, look at a fence post or rock at the end of the field that's in line with where you want to end up." I followed his advice, and the next time I plowed a straight furrow.

To me, this story serves as a great example of the value of having a clear vision. I see so many employees who execute their jobs while looking at the ground right in front of their feet. They understand what others want them to do, but they are not clearly focused on the end point. A vision is a clear picture of a desired future state. The purpose of a vision is to help employees set their direction and to provide a general heading. Vision is different from planning. Vision is designed to produce change, while a plan provides order for how things are to be accomplished. Having a good plan with no vision is like looking at the ground in front of the tractor.

Real change often begins as a recognition that a problem exists. Communication then can begin. People soon become clear about what they don't want. This is an important step in the process, but more important is the clear vision of where to go. Effective visions have the following characteristics:

- A vision is a destination, a place we want to go and not a place we want to avoid.
- Clarity is needed not only about what the destination is, but also about what it is not. Often it is just as important to describe where we are not going as where we want to go.
- Visions must be visual. People must be able to see the picture in their minds.
- Most visions begin as distant objects that can be seen, but they become much clearer and focused as you get closer.
- Visions are simple. A complex vision is difficult to clarify and often leads people in multiple directions.
- Clear visions can be communicated in less than five minutes.
- Exciting visions are mentioned often.
- Visions should be simplified to make them more realistic and attainable.
- Powerful visions often balance the interests of important constituencies.
- The best visions are consistent with other initiatives and strategies. If a new vision sends a different message than a previous vision, employees need to understand which is the correct message and why it has changed.

6. Communicating the Change

One of the most significant keys for implementing organizational change is communicating the change to employees throughout the organization. We often underestimate the need for constant communication, perhaps because we feel like we are repeating ourselves. This is true, but consider how we raise our children: Although we would like to believe that when we tell them something they will remember it for the rest of their lives, we learn by experience that we must find ways to reinforce important messages. When people don't hear messages for a long time, they tend to forget that the messages are important. A few keys for effectively communicating change include:

Talk about the change at every opportunity. When implementing a change, talk about it frequently.

Rely on face-to-face, one-on-one communication. Change starts at the grass roots, not in large meetings or company newsletters. Describing a change to a small group, face-to-face, provides the opportunity for dialog.

Use all available communications vehicles. Get the message out and then continue to repeat the message in multiple forms and formats.

Speak more with frontline supervisors and employees than with senior management. Senior managers need to be committed to making a change, but frequently they're already on board. Assuming the next level will fall in line with change efforts without any discussion or involvement is naive.

Focus on activities, not attitudes. Most change efforts begin with people who are not 100 percent on board. Typically, you hear negative comments, criticisms, and critiques. Focus on activities (what people are doing) rather than on attitudes (what people are saying). Attitudes soon fall in line with behaviors and activities.

Describe what should happen over the long term. In the beginning of change efforts, people often focus on activities or behaviors that need to be different. But focusing attention on these factors takes energy away from long-term visions. Remember, keep watching the fence post.

Communicate with energy. You are responsible not only for letting people know where the company is going, but also for getting them excited about going there. Excitement is contagious. I call this the Broadway dilemma. Most actors on Broadway want to star in a hit play, but the problem is that hit plays seem to go on for years. How can actors perform the same roles over and over, day after day, and still maintain enthusiasm for their job? The answer involves one of the secrets of change: To be successful, you must learn to maintain the same enthusiasm the first, the fiftieth, and the one-hundredth time you discuss your vision.

Communicate a sense of urgency. Letting people know that the change you are planning is important and needs special attention is critical to managing a successful change effort.

Articulate a feasible way to achieve the vision. All great journeys begin with the first step. Some visions paint a clear picture of the destination but provide only a sketchy map of how to get there. Communicate where to start. Communicate the first few months of activities and then tie them in to the final destination.

Articulate the vision stressing the values of the audience. People have different motives that influence their willingness to change. Clarify for different groups how a change ought to be communicated. Avoid selling or manipulation strategies; instead, describe change initiatives in language that fits your audience.

7. Moving from General to Specific

Change efforts often begin as very general recommendations. For example, we might say:

- "We need to improve the way we communicate."
- "Quality needs to be better."
- "We are not serving customers the way we should."

These general recommendations are great as a starting place for change. If, however, the suggestion for change remains general, then nothing is likely to change.

Gene Dalton found that to change, people must adjust their change plans from general terms to specific. General plans rarely lead to actual change because general plans and goals supply no specific actions to take. In fact, when organizations have only a general goal for change, no one knows how to take action to achieve the goal. Specific plans set the goals in motion and provide detailed, specific actions that lead to goal accomplishment.[1]

By keeping change plans general, organizations never have to change anything. The following conversation I had with my son, Brandon, about his grades, represents this idea:

"Son, what are your goals for your grades in school next semester?"

"I'm going to get better grades, Dad."

"How much better?"

"Oh, I don't know. But, you know, better than last semester."

"Does that mean a straight-A average?"

"No, not straight-As, Dad, but I'll do better. Can I go to Ben's house now?"

"First, tell me your goal. How much better are your grades going to be?"

"Just better, Dad. Why can't you just trust me to do better? Can I go to Ben's house now?"

By keeping the change goal general, Brandon didn't have to commit to anything. General goals do not lead to any specific behaviors, such as studying for three hours per night, having homework done before any other activities, turning in all assignments, doing well on all tests, doing extra-credit assignments, and retaking tests and assignments that resulted in low grades. Therefore, the odds of achieving the goal are greatly reduced.

General goals let us avoid the hassles of reality. But, by creating specific goals, we force ourselves to consider what it actually will take to change. Part of the movement from general goals to specific goals is deciding what we will do.

8. Learning from the Best

As organizations attempt significant change, they often find it difficult to know how to proceed and what to avoid. In most cases, the same changes have been made successfully by other organizations, and it can be helpful to benchmark against those organizations to help you understand what it takes. Many companies in the same industry will not allow specific benchmarking, but you can sometimes find organizations that are not competing with you for customers and that have been through similar experiences and have perhaps mastered some key skills for making a successful transition.

A petrochemical reseller was experiencing a significant shift in how its customers were purchasing products from distributors. To help the company understand how other organizations had handled significant changes in buying patterns and the effects of new technology, the company studied banks. With the influx of automated tellers, and with increased competition from other financial institutions, banks have had to make significant changes in how they work with customers and new technology. The petrochemical company's study was helpful in guiding its distributor through the complicated technological options and their implications.

Another company focused on improving its speed. The company defined speed as the time it took from taking an order to having the product installed. The benchmarking team decided to look at the difference between a typical garage and a garage specializing in oil changes in terms of the speed required for a typical oil change. The general garage required people to leave their cars for the entire day, but the specialty garage was able to change the oil and lubricate the car in 10 to 15 minutes while people waited. The specialty garage had specialized to the point that it only changed oil, while the garage handled a variety of repairs, many of which required lengthy processes. As the benchmarking team studied these companies, it quickly became evident that to improve speed, the company would need to reduce the product options offered to customers.

Our experience with benchmarking suggests that many companies are willing to take some time and share their learning with others. This can be an inexpensive way to obtain a great deal of knowledge quickly.

9. Defining Feedback Positively

In their book, *When Smart People Fail*, Carole Hyatt and Linda Gottlieb discuss the problems some successful people have when they encounter failure. When "failure makes us feel powerless and like a victim," change does not occur. They recommend that you "reinterpret your story" by casting your feedback in a more positive light, one in which you have more control.[2] Redefining negative feedback in a positive light creates increased motivation to change.

Engineers at a production plant were experiencing some significant reliability problems with the plant. Breakdowns would bring down the entire plant and cost as much as one million dollars per day. As maintenance engineers met to discuss the plant's reliability, it was clear that they felt at least partially responsible for the problem, but they also blamed many others who they felt contributed to the plant's poor reliability record. The plant was old, and cheap parts had been purchased to replace parts that were failing. Additionally, the problem-solving sessions held to discuss the breakdowns had typically turned into name-calling sessions, and few problems were solved in the meetings. Morale was low, people were frustrated, and nothing was changing. No one denied the problem, but no positive actions were being taken.

When things go wrong, we naturally assume defensive positions that do not facilitate change. Reviewing the problem, focusing on who was responsible and what action should be taken against whom, tends to paralyze people. The vision for change needs to be cast in a positive light. People need to know what to do, not what to avoid. In the

above example, the plant was able to identify three immediate actions that needed to take place. People were organized, plans were made, and action was begun. There was
very little resistance to the new programs, and they were
easily implemented.

10. Connecting Change with Company Culture

A company culture is the organization's way of thinking
and behaving. Within the company it seems natural and is
hardly noticeable. Typically, company culture is unwritten,
but it represents policy that can be very consistent and difficult to change.

A government contractor had built a factory to make computer chips. Because of the low volume of chips demanded by
the government for space exploration and high-tech equipment, the factory was not being used at full capacity. The
contractor decided to run some low-cost computer chips in
the factory to fill the unused capacity. The chips were already
designed and just needed to be manufactured. Soon, the contractor was producing the low-cost chips. Profit margins on
the low-cost chips were low, but because the infrastructure
and equipment were already in place, the contractor believed
it would be easy to make a profit.

After six months of production, the contractor reviewed
the profitability of the low-cost computer chips. The
accounting data indicated that the contractor was actually
losing money on every chip. When the reasons for the high
cost were examined, the contractor found that the factory
culture demanded extremely high quality. The facility typically manufactured high-tech computer chips designed for
space exploration, and so employees stressed high quality
because a failure in a computer chip in space could be cat-
astrophic. Both the company culture and the manufacturing process had been created based on high expectations
about quality. So, even though people knew the quality

specifications for the low-cost chips were much lower than usual, the contractor's culture led them to apply the same processes and approaches.

After the cost analysis, the contractor decided not to continue manufacturing the low-cost chips. The only way to make a profit on the chip would be to change the culture that reinforced the quality and effectiveness of the contractor's core product.

Each company must understand how intended changes will impact company culture. A common mistake in implementing change is that people see how another company has implemented a change and naturally believe, if they approach the change in the same way, the results will be the same. But, more often, the existing company culture significantly impacts how changes are implemented.

One company was trying to improve quality. A root-cause analysis revealed that total-quality initiatives were being impeded by the company culture, which centered on doing whatever customers wanted. Employees prided themselves on accomplishing the impossible for their customers. For example, if an employee specified a time of delivery, and the customer asked for delivery in half that time, the employee would still find a way to accomplish the task in half the time. Praise and recognition would be heaped on the employee by the customer. Occasionally, however, errors accompanied these Herculean efforts. The errors, though small, were viewed very negatively by customers.

Company managers decided to set realistic time frames for delivery and then stand by them. Customer service representatives were instructed, "Just tell them 'no.' " But customers were not used to hearing "No." It didn't sound like the same company anymore. Other companies could stick to their deadlines, and for some reason it wasn't viewed by customers as negative. But the feedback from customers on the company's new policy was very negative. Also, employees didn't like to say, "No." It felt like they were not serving their customers as well. And even though employees had been given clear instructions on realistic time frames, the practice continued.

The company's change process ultimately was very difficult. Customers had to be educated that error-free work was more important to them than a few weeks' turnaround. The company lost a few customers, but most customers began to plan their jobs better and the more realistic timing was built into their processes. Employees attended several training sessions that stressed the value of quality. Employees soon began to see that delivering a product in half the time but with errors was not serving the customer.

11. Practicing

We would never consider coaching an athletic team without scheduling time to practice. We wouldn't assume that people on the team would naturally know how to work together, or that every member of the team had the skills to execute plays well. New skills, new teams, and different approaches require practice. We should not expect performance to be high at first. New teams need good coaching, feedback, skill-building drills, and practice.

Sometimes, practicing change is fairly straightforward; at other times, we may not know how to practice. Here are a few practice tips:

1. Have the team read an article or book.

2. Hold a training course on new skills required for the change.

3. Provide team members with instructional audio tapes.

4. Hold regular staff meetings and review the change process. Talk about successes, failures, and exceptional efforts. Role-play different situations.

5. Share your learning with other teams going through the same change.

6. Assign outside coaches or mentors to teams to help them work through difficult problems.

7. Organize field trips to visit other organizations that have mastered the skills or experiences your team needs.

8. Find ways to measure, implement, and keep track of progress.

9. Look for off-line opportunities to practice. Members of the team might get involved in community service or extra-curricular activities to help them build required skills.

10. Look at systems and processes that support the change and those that distract from the change.

11. Recognize aspects of the company culture that make change difficult and brainstorm ways to integrate the change into the culture.

12. Be patient but persistent. Change takes time, but it also takes continued effort.

12. Avoiding Belief Traps

A building supply company made tubs and shower enclosures used primarily in new residential construction. In an effort to shore up their market share, the company conducted interviews with its 40 contractors. Prior to the interviews, the company also interviewed "internal customers," the employees who worked with contractors. As a group, the building contractors were characterized as unorganized and demanding. Stories circulated about how contractors would forget to order materials and then call up the same day materials were needed, demanding that something be installed.

On the other hand, interviews with building contractors seemed to highlight the complexity of their work. Contractors were expected to coordinate the efforts of several different subcontractors in a short period of time to produce a finished home on time with high quality. Some of the interviews with contractors were conducted over the phone, often either late at night or early in the morning when the contractors were in their home offices. The contractors seemed to be master jugglers who were very good at keeping dozens of projects going all at once.

After the interviews, the company constructed a profile to outline the average workday of a building contractor. It was frantic. When the profile was presented to employees, it was easy for them to see why contractors might frequently order late and be demanding. The employees were asked, "If you were a contractor, what kind of performance would you expect from your best subcontractors?" The employees answered that top subcontractors would need to be dependable, reliable, and responsive to short deadlines.

One employee suggested, "If I were a contractor, I would really value subcontractors that made my job and life easier. I have always thought the problem with most contractors was that they're not organized, and it must have been their own fault if they didn't get what they needed when they needed it. If a subcontractor came to me and said he or she would help me plan and order materials for each house, track progress, and oversee the installation, I would give that subcontractor all my business because it would make my life so much easier. If we did that for our contractors, our business would run much more efficiently, and we would get more business. The time it takes to plan for them would be less than the time it takes for us to react to their emergencies."

Until employees had changed the way they thought about contractors, nothing would have changed in the customer relationship. But, by changing their thinking, many of the employees were able to build stronger relationships with contractors and improve their business.

In their book *Prisoners of Belief,* Matthew McKay and Patrick Fanning indicate that core beliefs "define how you feel about yourself and the emotional tone of your life."[3] Our beliefs include our feelings about our competence and abilities, attitudes about other people, stereotypes, values, and motives.

One of the employee beliefs was that contractors were "unorganized and demanding." This belief was maintained by a process called selective attention—only paying attention to events that support our belief system and ignoring those that don't. McKay and Fanning call this "mental grooving," falling into a rut that makes it easier to deal with people and situations. We can break free from some of these self-defeating beliefs by first understanding our core beliefs and the rules associated with those beliefs. Changing our behavior often requires changing our core beliefs.

We can also go through the process of testing our beliefs in an objective way. When we test our beliefs, we often recognize that our rigid personal rules are not true. In the above case, as employees began to better understand the difficult work the contractors had, it was no longer surprising that contractors might occasionally forget to order materials.

Finally, we can develop new beliefs that support and reinforce positive behavior. A psychological disorder called "imagined ugliness" (body dimorphic disorder) shows how this works. People with this disorder imagine they are ugly when they are not. These people focus extensively on small defects and exaggerate them: "My hands and fingers don't look right." They focus all their attention on small, irrelevant things. Therapy to help these individuals focuses on teaching them to be more objective and realistic in their evaluations.

As you introduce a new change in an organization, ask yourself and others, "What beliefs, values, or rules do we have that *do not* support and reinforce what I am attempting to change?" Sometimes, to make a change in an organization, you must change common beliefs.

13. Shaping Goals and Behaviors

Sometimes organizations try to change things so complex or unique that the organization has little skill, experience, or expertise to complete the change. For example, an organization that had not used much technology in the past (e-mail, Internet, databases, or scheduling software) might try to change to incorporate the technology in all areas. But it may be difficult for the company to succeed with such a comprehensive change in the short term. The company could hire an information systems professional to help, but that person can't make employees use the new systems. If organizations do not currently have the skills or expertise, they may find it difficult even to begin the change process. This is when shaping becomes helpful.

I first encountered "shaping" in an animal behavior class in college. I was assigned to train a rat to press a lever to get water. The animals had been deprived of water and then placed in the training cage with the lever. I waited patiently for the rat to press the lever, but it never even went close to the lever. By the end of the lab period, the rat was still thirsty, and it had made no attempt to press the lever. I felt very discouraged.

Then I learned about shaping. In shaping behavior, you reward successive approximations of a desired behavior. During the next lab period, I began by giving the rat a drink as soon as it turned toward the lever. Although turning toward the lever was not the final, desired result of pressing the lever, I couldn't train the rat to press the lever unless it got close to it. However, I could reward the rat for looking or moving in the right direction until it learned where the lever was.

Soon the rat began to turn quickly toward the lever. I would wait for the rat to turn and approach the lever before I rewarded it. I was amazed at how fast the shaping process worked. By the end of the second session the rat busily pressed the lever whenever it wanted water.

Organizational shaping is somewhat different from teaching tricks to rats, but the same principle applies. For some systems and processes, incremental change can create substantial change over time.

James Brian Quinn coined the phrase "logical incrementalism." Logical incrementalism means that organizations take small, incremental steps to achieve change.[4] Many organizations talk about frame-breaking change, but frame-breaking change is the opposite of logical incrementalism. Frame-breaking change means that everything totally changes overnight. Sometimes frame-breaking change does not work. It can destroy the culture and trust of an organization. But incrementalism, or organizational shaping, begins the change process with incremental steps.

In the technology example at the beginning of this section, the company might begin by getting everyone a computer. Then, after a few months it could install e-mail and a scheduling software program. After training the employees on how to use their computers, e-mail, and software, some of the employees may begin to use the new technology and incorporate it into their jobs. These employees can then become coaches and mentors to others. In one such example, a company went from being technologically backward to being a technology leader in a little over three years. By using an incremental approach to change, the company encountered little resistance to change. Also, the company saved money because the longer they waited, the lower the cost of the software and hardware.

One warning about incrementalism: Many organizations use an incremental approach to change, but they never really change. The technique can be used to avoid making difficult decisions and to slow down when a fast move may be preferred. Incrementalism can make you feel like you're changing, but it can be mistaken for real change. In these cases, incrementalism is more like slow death than change.

14. Rewarding Change Efforts

As you try to implement changes, ask yourself if rewarding employee behavior or results will help implement a change. Too often, we embrace change for its own sake. Managers seem to believe that employees naturally want to change. Employees ask themselves, but never vocalize, things such as, "What is in this for me?" Keep in mind that rewards are not only money. Recognition, praise, competition, rewarding work, career opportunities, and new challenges often work as effectively as money. Some steps for linking rewards to change efforts include:

1. Determine desired outcomes. Be clear about desired outcomes. Set short-term, intermediate, and final outcomes before beginning change efforts. At first it may seem obvious, but many desired outcomes are difficult to quantify and measure. Such difficult-to-measure efforts may involve improving collaboration between groups or increasing communication up and down the organization.

2. Find ways to measure or evaluate outcomes. Some things are easy to measure: profitability, waste, output, head count, and costs; other things are more difficult, such as intuitive or subjective judgments. For example, team effectiveness could be measured by having an objective committee evaluate each team.

3. Test the measurement system. Whenever there is a direct link between performance and rewards, make sure the measurement system is reliable. Look for ways people might manipulate the system to get desired rewards.

4. Brainstorm potential rewards. Don't assume money is the only way to motivate people. Brainstorm potential rewards and then match up rewards to different groups of people. Technical employees, for example, may be rewarded with new equipment while front-line employees may prefer time off.

5. Link outcomes and rewards. Once you determine the outcomes and rewards, decide next how to link them. Rewards can be linked in a fixed or variable fashion. Fixed rewards occur at specified intervals or at the occurrence of an outcome, such as sales commissions or profit sharing. Variable rewards occur more randomly, such as recognition of superb individual performance. With variable rewards, people may not get recognized every time they perform, but occasional recognition can be effective in reinforcing behavior. An example of a variable reward is occasionally buying lunch for a group of employees. At lunch, link the reward (lunch) to several outcomes that were achieved in recent months.

6. Communicate or demonstrate. Typically, fixed rewards require specific and detailed communication. People need to know "the rules of the game and how to play." Variable rewards can be demonstrated, such as recognizing people when you see the desired behavior, without being formally communicated.

7. Follow through. Research has shown that variable rewards tend to produce longer-lasting effects. But the problem with variable rewards is that it's easy to forget and allow the rewards to drop off. It's important to follow through until the change is well-established.

Caution: Rewards can be powerful. Keep the following rule in mind when establishing fixed rewards linked to pay: "It's easy to give, but hard to take away." The following additional guidelines may help you establish a reward program without violating employee expectations:

1. Be clear about the reward period. Is the reward program for one year or forever?

2. Make sure your reward program is not set in concrete. Communicate up front with employees that you anticipate some modifications in the reward system. In a recent survey we evaluated a facility's gain-sharing program. One group was very negative about the program because it appeared to be impossible to achieve the gain-sharing reward. To make the plan fair, it needed to be calibrated.

3. Don't be too generous. Over-rewarding can teach you a tough lesson. Once when I was trying to get one of my children to read more, I offered one dollar for every book he read. I saw no change. I went to five dollars and still he didn't read, nor did he read when I raised the reward to seven dollars. At the ten-dollar level he read 20 books in two months.

4. Look for negative side effects of rewards. People learn quickly. If you reward them for outcome A and not for outcome B, then, unless outcome B is a natural consequence of outcome A, you will get less of outcome B.

5. Be fair. Rewards can be morale killers for people that get left out. I find that nothing frustrates people more than when they work hard only to see others get the recognition.

15. Creating Structure to Support Change

I travel every week. In the past, I would go to the airport, park my car, and then run to catch my flight. A few days later when I returned I could never remember where I'd parked my car. I would eventually find the car, but it would sometimes take as much as 20 minutes of walking up and down the aisles to find it. This became very frustrating for me, especially at the end of long trips, and I had a great desire to change.

I remember trying several different techniques: I would try to make a mental picture of the area so I would remember it; or I would write down the row number on my parking ticket. These techniques seemed to work as long as I wasn't in a hurry, in which cases I was more worried about missing my plane than about remembering where I'd parked my car. Finally, I came across a structural solution to solve my problem. I found an area of the parking lot where I knew I could always find a place in approximately the same location every time. Now, although it's a little farther away, I can always remember where I'm parked. I don't have to worry about it anymore. And although my memory is not any better, I no longer have to remember. It always works.

Creating change in an organization is like walking a high-wire tightrope without a net. Creating structure to support change efforts is like adding a net, a balancing stick, and ropes on both sides to hang on to—just in case. Structure makes weak organizations strong and strong organizations stable. Like a large building, once structure is established, if you remove the structure the building collapses. By framing proposed changes within a structured environment, most changes are easier to execute.

Structure includes systems, processes, procedures, and approaches that facilitate change. (Figure 9.1 provides a list of structured and unstructured approaches to change efforts.)

Information technology is now on the cutting edge for creating new systems and processes that can dramatically impact change efforts. For example, e-mail provides companies with the ability to communicate more quickly and at a lower cost than ever before.

Change Effort	*Unstructured Approach*	*Structured Approach*
Exercise at least three times per week.	Set a goal and write it down on paper.	Hire a trainer; buy exercise equipment; instruct trainer to come to your house and pull you out of bed if necessary.
Hold regular staff meetings.	Encourage groups to meet more often; set goals for how often the group should meet.	Schedule all group meetings for the year; have all group members include the schedule in their personal calendars.
Improve collaboration between groups.	Ask groups to collaborate and to give an occasional speech about the value of collaboration.	Set up monthly meetings between groups where collaborations must occur; ask them to share positive and negative feedback; reward groups who collaborate best.

Figure 9.1: Creating structure to support change.

Recently, one of my partners described a new client of ours from Greece. The client had purchased our product, but he had never physically met my partner or anyone at our company. I asked how he had made the sale. He told me that, because of the time difference, they had only spoken on the phone once, but he had managed the sales process through e-mail. Having been an editor for the *Wall Street Journal*, he could quickly compose compelling and informative e-mail messages.

Likewise, an intranet offers companies the ability to share information and provide a method of common access in the company. Sophisticated applications facilitate product ordering, customer service, billing, help systems, and analysis systems. This new information technology creates a tremendous advantage for those who learn how to take advantage of the technology. As you begin the change process, ask yourself how information technology could help you.

Many organizations are also experimenting with new organizational charts to facilitate change. Traditional company functions (R&D, Sales, Manufacturing) are being replaced by new, cross-functional structures. These new structures can facilitate change. The new structures change the way people look at the world, the way people interact with others, and the way decisions are made. The new structures also change many traditional notions that employees have about careers, promotions, and development. (In traditional systems, functional specialists are promoted for functional expertise, but in the new systems, general skills are more highly valued, although there is less opportunity for promotion.) Also, if you can align the organizational structure with the change process, you may find changes are easier to execute. Keep in mind, however, structural changes also impact many other systems and processes in the organization.

16. Building Organizational Confidence

Scott Adams, creator of "Dilbert," has been phenomenally popular lately. Part of the reason for his cartoon's popularity is that Adams is very clever and creative. Many of his cartoons carry an underlying theme that I personally identify with, and I think others do, too. This underlying theme is that, in general, organizations don't care about people. This theme suggests that organizational programs, changes, and processes typically benefit the organization, and especially upper management, rather than the average employee. I think Scott Adams has done a great job of capturing the cynicism many feel toward organizations. I don't think Adams created Dilbert's cynicism, but he acts as a sort of therapeutic spokesman for many.

The cynicism that people hold toward companies is well-deserved by those companies. For the most part, organizations have fought for survival at the expense of many people. Organizations we once knew as career companies, where a person could work for an entire career, have either disappeared or destroyed the loyalty they once enjoyed.

Undertaking a change effort in an organization typically requires the commitment and involvement of employees. Often, employees are told how the new program will benefit them. Most employees probably greet this approach with some cynicism. It has become the exception rather than the rule that employees are not skeptical of change efforts. The following recommendations may help organizations deal with employee cynicism and foster employee confidence in company change efforts.

Anticipate cynicism. Cynicism is inevitable.

Don't underestimate cynicism. Employees have great expertise in passive resistance (saying the right things but doing nothing to help). Cynicism can kill a good change effort.

Be realistic. What impact will change efforts really have on employees? Any program that improves organizational efficiency typically results in a smaller work force. Employees know this will happen. Be clear about how and when reductions will occur.

Have good answers. Tell people the truth. They can handle it, and you will be respected. If you're the messenger, then push management to provide clear answers.

Involvement is key. Employees tend to be less cynical about programs and changes they are involved in creating.

Walk in their shoes. Will this change process pass your most cynical test? If not, don't do it. Employees aren't stupid. You may fool them once, but never twice.

17. Involving Individuals in Organizational Change

Often, managers who initiate organizational change don't fully recognize that for the change to be achieved, individuals must change their behavior. This is always implied but rarely explicit. Change efforts work best when individuals know what is expected. Individual expectations often are not clarified because they are not understood. When change efforts and goals remain at a global, general level, the individual changes required are never explicit. For example, if an organization is working to improve collaboration between groups, then the organization needs to define the individual behaviors to facilitate that collaboration. Making those behaviors explicit to employees and incorporating the employees into feedback and appraisal processes helps to reinforce the organizational change.

A fast-food restaurant chain conducted a cultural assessment and found three issues that needed immediate attention and change. The worldwide parent company established an action plan to create change in the overall organization. After evaluating the plan, directors asked, "If we successfully executed this action plan at the parent-company level, would that be enough to create the needed change?" The answer, of course, was "No."

Everyone in the company felt that many aspects of the problem existed at all levels and locations of the organization. A plan was created to share the results of the cultural assessment throughout the organization in a planning session for company supervisors. Each person in the session would be asked to develop an individual action plan to address the three issues in their work group.

At the work group level, the assessment results were then presented by the supervisor, and each individual was asked to create a development plan for one of the three issues on which they could take personal action. Driving the same three issues to every level of the organization, creating both the systems and the structural changes, along with individual behavioral changes made for a substantial difference in the company's performance in the three issues.

Focusing on individual behavior impacts organizational change from two perspectives: One, if companies can get their organizational structure right, and align it with their strategy and systems, then people will adapt their behavior to those conditions; on the other hand, if companies can influence individuals to modify their behavior appropriately and then create systems and structures to support those behaviors, then the organization can change more quickly. In reality, both perspectives are true. Individuals find it easier to change when systems and processes are in place. But if they aren't in place, individuals may be lead or persuaded to fully utilize whatever systems and structures are in place.

18. Keeping the Effort Alive

One problem with change efforts is they are easier to start than to finish. Pushing change efforts to completion requires both persistence and patience. The following list of tips and hints may help you keep your change efforts going:

Be realistic when you start by acknowledging that you will need to reinvigorate your efforts. When planning your change effort, consider how to keep it going by:

– Checking progress.
– Reporting on partial progress.
– Creating events to motivate people.
– Communicating frequently and consistently.

Don't get upset when things stall. It's normal for change efforts to stall occasionally, but have a plan to restart your effort. Often, this shows employees that you are really serious about this change.

Generate short-term wins. Break a big change effort down into smaller wins that can be celebrated and acknowledged.

Don't stop pushing too soon or the organization will revert back. Employees learn to say the right things before the change is in cement. Some changes are like bad habits that come back if constant attention is not paid to the change.

Put systems, processes, and procedures in place to support and reinforce the change effort.

Find natural opportunities to review progress on changes, such as quarterly meetings or even annual events.

Talk about your successes and remind employees about the additional effort required for success.

19. Empowering Employees

Norman Smallwood, one of my partners, told me about an R&D lab for a large paper company that had empowered its employees at all levels with a clear knowledge of the company's strategy and how the company could gain a competitive advantage by executing the strategy well. Managers from another company came to visit to observe the implementation of the strategy. After it was briefed, the group was invited on a tour of the facility. At the conclusion of the tour, the group gathered in the lobby. A few visitors became separated from the main group at the elevator, and, as they were waiting for the next one, they conversed with one of the employees who was also waiting.

They quizzed the employee about the company's strategy and why changes were so critical to the company's success. The visitors were quite impressed with his answers and the enthusiasm he demonstrated. After rejoining the rest of the group, the visitors who had been separated asked the host if he knew the employee they had spoken with on their trip down. "Yes," replied the host, "Robert is a wonderful employee." The group asked what Robert's job was in the facility. "Oh," replied the host, "he's a janitor."

In a group meeting following the trip, group members were asked what impressed them the most about their visit. The consensus was, "Robert, the Janitor." The group of managers felt that if all employees understood and were committed to the company's strategy, even down to the janitor, imagine the power an organization would have to execute that strategy.

With clear leadership, employees at all levels of the organization can be advocates for change. Some leaders find the process of creating change to be a lonely process. They feel both isolated and unsupported. Most of the time, these leaders are also unsuccessful. For organizations to function effectively with leaner, flatter structures, employees at the bottom must be given additional influence and control. In the old command-and-control organizations, a few committed managers with a common shared vision could create change. But in today's lean, flat organizations, more people need to be committed to change efforts.

Employees at all levels not only need to be committed, but they also need to be knowledgeable. They need to see what the leaders see, understand what the leaders understand, and be as committed to the change as the leaders are. With employees at all levels focused on the same future, there can be tremendous power and great potential.

20. Making Tradeoffs

Most of the time, significant changes require some tradeoffs. The basic notion of tradeoffs is that, in order for a company to make a change, they must give up something. The following case illustrates this point:

A small service organization felt it had been spending excessively and it was time to tighten the company's belts. All the key executives were present when the management group decided to take a hard look at the company's spending practices. Soon, a study was conducted, and recommendations were made that would result in major savings and improved profits. The executives met again to review the findings.

As the first recommendations were reviewed, the executives as a group responded positively to the changes. The first recommendations focused on changes at lower levels of the organization. But the next set of recommendations focused on issues with executives. Executives were not spending within their budgets, and some of the expenses were questionably of a personal nature. The executives all had personal assistants, and one recommendation focused on cutting the amount of personal assistance in half. The executives became very defensive, claiming the spending level was a necessity. After some time, the executives began to see that, to control spending, each would have to make some personal sacrifices.

Once companies are clear about the changes they really want, they must also clarify the tradeoffs necessary to make those changes happen. You can rarely have it all, and, most of the time, to get one thing we really want we must give up something else.

21. Focusing

Finally, organizations and individuals can pay attention only to a limited number of things at one time. Introducing too many initiatives, activities, or projects can divert the attention and effectiveness of an organization. Managers must act as gate keepers to limit the competing priorities allowable for the organization or group and each person in it. Most gate keepers, of course, try to eliminate "bad" initiatives or activities. But what they soon find is that very few initiatives or activities are "bad." Most seem to be good things to do, but there still are too many. The more activities allowed in your organization, the greater the distraction from the core activities that create competitive advantage.

The following list of tips can help you eliminate unwanted initiatives and activities.

• Is this activity linked directly to the core mission of your organization?

• If the organization were to focus its attention on this activity, is there evidence that the effectiveness or efficiency of accomplishing the core mission would improve?

• If you are required to do the activity because of a corporate mandate, and the activity is not directly linked to the company's core mission, find ways to minimize the distraction caused by the activity.

• Decide on a limited number of "charity" or "good corporate citizen" projects to be completed in one year. Once you select those projects, explain to those who continue to solicit your help that you officially sponsor only a tiny number of activities per year, and that you have already selected those activities.

• Annually review the activities and initiatives of your organization. Most organizations find up to 50 percent of their activities add no value to the company. Eliminate activities that add no value and focus on activities that add value.

In this chapter, 21 different recommendations were presented on how to create change in organizations. If anyone tries to do all 21, I predict their change efforts will be unsuccessful. We have found that, depending on the change your organization is going through and the culture of your organization, using a few of these suggestions at a time will help you to produce change.

Notes to Chapter Nine

1. Gene Dalton, Louis B. Barnes and Abraham Zaleznik, *The Distribution of Authority in Formal Organizations,* Boston, MA: Division of Research, Harvard Business School, 1968, Chapter 5: "Change in Organizations" (Reprinted: Boston, MA: MIT Press, 1973).

2. Carole Hyatt and Linda Gottlieb, *When Smart People Fail: Rebuilding Yourself for Success,* New York: Penguin Books, 1987.

3. Matthew McKay and Patrick Fanning, *Prisoners of Belief: Exposing & Changing Beliefs That Control Your Life,* Oakland, CA: New Harbinger, 1991.

4. James Brian Quinn, *Strategies for Change: Logical Incrementalism,* Homewood, IL: Richard D. Irwin, 1980.

CHAPTER TEN

Leading Change

As organizations struggle to change, one critical ingredient remains unchallenged as a driving source for creating meaningful change: leadership. Leadership is the ability to get an organization excited, motivated, committed, and to get it to perform in new and better ways, and it is a critical skill that can't be replaced in any successful change effort.

Leading change is partly genetic and partly learned and developed. In this chapter I present ten characteristics of effective leadership that differentiates effective leaders from ineffective leaders. These characteristics are keys that, if developed, can assist leaders in managing the change process.

The Executive Study

Recently, 275 executives received multi-rater assessment surveys. The surveys contained 98 questions asking for written comments on the leader's strengths and weaknesses. The survey measured 23 dimensions of executive behavior:

- Vision, monitoring the environment
- Distinctive competence and communication of direction
- Directive leadership
- Managing commitments
- Risk-taking
- Meeting commitments
- Organization
- Incrementalism, managing ambiguity
- Personal competence
- Building competence
- Building trust
- Confrontation
- Exercising influence
- Consideration

- Integrity
- Making tough decisions
- Getting results
- Persuasion
- Representing

- Networking
- Availability
- Sponsoring
- Managing diversity

The executives distributed 12 surveys to their direct reports, peers, and bosses, and then completed one survey on themselves. When the surveys were completed, the 15 highest-scoring executives were compared to the 15 lowest-scoring executives using the 98-item survey as a measure of overall effectiveness. T-tests were computed to help understand which survey items best differentiated the highest- from the lowest-scoring individuals. Written comments were also reviewed for both groups to understand how high- and low-scoring executives were described. The items that best discriminated between high- and low-scoring executives were then factor-analyzed to create major clusters or factors.

The Problem with Conventional Wisdom

I recently read an article that advised executives on how to be more effective. The article recommended that executives arrive on time for meetings and appointments. Being late was described as a critical mistake that would hurt a person's overall effectiveness. I found that interesting because, in our study, we found an item that measured how often executives were late for appointments and meetings. We found that effective executives were no more likely to be rated highly for being on time than ineffective executives. This validated my own experience. Some of the best leaders I know are often late for meetings, and some of the worst leaders I know are always on time. Other effective leaders are on time, and poor leaders seem to be late. But the point is that the tendency to be on time or late is not correlated with overall effectiveness. On the other hand, our study did, in fact, indicate which factors make the most difference. Of the 23 dimensions and 98 items researched, we determined that ten are key to leadership effectiveness.

Ten Differentiating Factors

The following ten factors were determined to be key differentiators between the best and worst leaders:
- Getting results
- Integrity: walking your talk
- Trust and respect
- Vision and confidence in the future
- Organization
- Persuasion
- Inspiration
- Innovation and experimentation
- Analytical, technical competence
- People skills and consideration

1. Getting results. The best executives under "getting results" were described as follows:
- They play key roles in helping work units meet their deadlines.
- They are highly committed to meeting organizational goals and objectives.
- They have a can-do, never-say-die attitude.
- They make things happen rather than letting them happen.

A comment described one of the best executives in the following way, "He gives 100 percent of himself. He doesn't know everything, but he will help find a solution every time." The worst executives were seen as "letting things happen" or "accepting good enough as good enough." The worst executives were told they needed to "step up and take charge," and that too often they were "satisfied with slipshod work."

The best executives in our study knew the difference between driving for activity and driving for results. Driving for activity is keeping people busy, while driving for results keeps people focused on delivering key results: a huge and important distinction. People who scored high on driving for results were not afraid to push for higher levels of effort and production than people who generally felt comfortable. The key to keeping employees performing at high levels is to get employees to push themselves for higher effort rather than having managers push them.

2. Integrity: Walking your talk. Those who "walked their talk" were perceived more positively than those who couldn't be trusted or who had questionable integrity. Executives with high integrity were described as follows:

- They are trusted to not take advantage of people or the organization.
- They do not use coercive or position power to get what they want.
- They never cause others to question the executives' integrity because of actions.
- They are honest in their dealings with others.
- They practice what they preach.
- They never say one thing and do another.

Written comments described the best executives as: "Stands up for his employees, always, even when we're wrong. He'll take the blame, and he never blames us when things go wrong." "He has the highest integrity and commitment of any manager in the company." "His integrity is unquestionable. I have never seen it waiver."

The worst executives were described in the opposite way: "When things go wrong, she fingers the blame on subordinates." "Does not practice what he preaches. He parrots his boss, but doesn't believe in it." "He's too political to have integrity." "I question her integrity because of her overriding sense that her primary objective is to promote herself." "He is wishy-washy, bouncing back and forth between differing arguments."

Integrity is a key behavior of effective leaders. We are quick to judge our leaders' integrity. Integrity is difficult to maintain all the time. Any slight indiscretion can often be perceived as a total loss. Working issues to make them politically correct is also typically seen as a loss of integrity. Integrity is easy to lose and difficult to regain in the perceptions of others.

3. Trust and respect. Executives are judged as trusted and respected based on hundreds, or even thousands, of actions and interactions over time. Integrity helps build trust, and good business competence and technical skills help build others' confidence in executive judgment. The best executives under "trust and respect" were described by others as follows:

- Others have confidence in their business judgment.
- They are respected and trusted by those with whom they work.
- They build up credit and trust with others in the organization.

Written comments described the best executives as: "Fair, understanding, and trusted." "Trusted totally." "He's the most trustworthy person in the company." "Very high level of trust; can keep confidences." "Never has given a reason to inspire anything but absolute trust."

The worst executives were described with the following comments: "He is insincere. There's usually a gap between his real and declared aims, necessitating the use of long words and exhaustive idioms. There is always a hidden agenda in dealing with him." "He isn't to be trusted. He tries to hide things and then springs them on people. Often, he contradicts previous communications." "Not much trust.

People know it doesn't take much from management to have him change his position." "Trust can't be commanded. It needs to be earned from each individual." "There is a sense of mistrust for him throughout the community." "He is primarily concerned with promoting himself."

4. Vision and confidence in the future. There's a difference between doing work and working to achieve a vision. "Doing work" is activity, while "working to achieve a vision" is results. The key to delivering results versus activity is vision. The best executives have a clear vision and can share that vision with others. The worst executives have goals, objectives, and work, but they have little vision. The best executives were described as follows:

- They provide a definite sense of direction and purpose.
- They have a clear vision of the future of this organization.
- They make others feel this company is going someplace.

Written comments described high performers as follows: "Continually provides updated clarification." "Has frequent staff meetings to keep us all focused in one direction." "Is always the optimist, tries to stay one step ahead by looking at long-range plans." "He not only articulates well the end objectives of the organization, but also the methods and mechanisms needed to achieve them."

Written comments on the worst executives indicated: "Needs to work on strategic planning: Where are we going?" "There is a great amount of frustration caused by his ever-changing clear vision." "Direction is provided from the bottom up ('You guys know where we need to go')." "Seems satisfied to let others decide the role of his organization." "Tries to communicate a vision, but he comes across as insincere and aloof."

Those who lack vision do so because they lack clear understanding of products and the needs and concerns of customers. They lack the breadth of understanding needed to provide a broad perspective. They may have in-depth views about one aspect of the business, but that doesn't make them a visionary. They lack energy and initiative to engage others in conversations that lead to in-depth visions rather than rehearsed paragraphs created by upper management.

5. Organization. The best executives are jugglers. They keep 50 balls in the air at once and rarely drop one. The ability to organize activities quickly, use brevity, and manage time is a key skill of the best executives. The best executives were described as follows:

- They are organized and know what to do next.
- They don't waste time on matters of low importance or value.
- They anticipate problems and work on them before they become a crisis.
- They spend enough time with those they work with.

Written comments of the best executives described them as: "He is always on top of things, both efficient and punctual, never flustered." "Has a good vision in identifying priorities." "Excellent time management skills." "Organized, efficient, and punctual." "Seems to utilize his direct reports and administrative staff well. Items do not back up on his desk."

The worst performers were described differently: "His nickname is 'Captain Chaos.'" "Loosely organized." "Creates the impression of going in many different directions at once." "Unorganized and inefficient. Often assigns single projects to multiple people only to end up with overlapping efforts."

6. Persuasion. The best executives have the ability to persuade others to accept their position. It takes skill to generate a clear vision, but the key to effectiveness is persuading others that your vision is correct. Delivering results is a key attribute, but the ability to persuade others to deliver excellent results is a critical characteristic of effective executives. High-performing executives were described as follows:

- They are able to clearly articulate their positions.
- They are able to persuade others to accept their positions.
- They have a personal style that helps win others over to their positions.
- They are able to represent the organization to critical groups outside the organization.
- They present an appropriate company image both inside and outside the organization.
- They champion projects so others understand and support them.

Written comments on the best group of executives expressed a very positive view of their abilities to persuade others: "Able to convey the most complex issues in simple terms." "Easily persuades those who are easily swayed, and sometimes persuades even the most opinionated." "Wins people over many times with sheer enthusiasm." "He persuades with hard-core data, facts, figures, and past experience, not with 'hunches' or 'gut feelings.'"

Written comments for the worst executives showed low ability to persuade others: "Is not effective at persuasion. Lacks diplomacy, tends to be confrontational and emotional." "Very strong and emotional at times. Tends to dictate." "Likable, but not persuasive." "He gets his way by ordering, but I don't think he can persuade a worker or a peer." "Rarely clearly articulates his position."

7. Inspiration. The best executives lift others above what is normal or ordinary, get people to do more than they thought possible, build people up, and get people excited. The best executives are inspirational, not merely transactional. The best executives were described as follows:

- They energize people to go the extra mile.

• They inspire people to care about and strive for excellent performance.

Written comments described the best performers as: "Leads through his own example." "He inspires confidence." "There is no one I know that doesn't have confidence in him."

The worst performers were described very differently. It was evident from written comments that people could be very clear about what inspiration is not: "He seems to have plateaued or 'burned-out' in his job. He seems tired of management problems, challenges, and changes." "I believe he is competent, but he comes across as a 'bean-counter' and 'nitpicker'; he doesn't inspire or motivate those who work with him." "He operates on the 'I'm the boss' principle, which doesn't work." "When backed up by resistance, he often relies on 'that's the way the big guy wants it.'" "He relies on his physical properties—his voice and size." "Makes people feel unimportant."

8. Innovation and experimentation. Most executives face many challenges. Simply "working harder" will not solve those challenges. There simply isn't enough time in the day or night to hit the aggressive targets that most executives are given. The best executives work smarter, not just harder. The smart part of their job involves finding ways to do work differently. Innovation is the key to future success. Successful executives who think outside the box and pursue new and different ideas are described as follows:

• They constructively challenge others to question the usual way of looking at things.

Written comments describe the best innovative executives as: "Imaginative solutions." "Always pushing and encouraging others to find ways to do things better." "Refuses to accept 'it's always been done this way' as an adequate reason to do something." "Willing to bend the rules."

The worst performers were described very differently: "Has an aversion to trying new ideas unless he can be certain of the outcome; this causes frustration among subordinates." "Rarely looks at ideas unless they are shoved down his throat!" "Comes from the 'don't rock the boat' school of thought."

9. *Analytical, technical competence.* The ability of executives to understand technical issues is critical in the success of many organizations. We admire executives who can provide a simple yet comprehensive vision of the future. That simple vision is constructed after a thorough analysis of facts, figures, and projections. The best executives have the ability both to comprehend technical and financial data quickly and to formulate insightful conclusions that lead the organization forward. The best executives are described as follows:

- They are able to make effective business decisions based on an excellent understanding of financial, economic, market, and organizational data.
- They make decisions that reflect an understanding of the needs of the total business rather than the needs of small parts of the organization.
- They do not seek quick-fix solutions to complex problems when more understanding and study are needed.

Written comments describe these executives as: "Very competent; has the respect of his work unit as well as the organization." "Quick comprehension and assimilation of complex situations." "There is no questioning his competence. He possesses one of the brightest analytical minds in his profession." "Has demonstrated his ability to deal with the most complicated issues."

The worst executives were described in a very negative light: "Sometimes goes off half-cocked." "Persons in this work unit, right down to the clerks, have absolutely no confidence in his abilities or competence."

10. People skills and consideration. The final skill in which the best executives show substantially more ability than the worst executives is "people skills and consideration." Even though it is listed last, it is not the least important. The ability to understand the needs and concerns of others, to listen, and to act considerately are huge assets for any executive. Many people think they have these skills, but the only way to know is to be evaluated by others. Some people see this competency as opposite of the drive for results, but it's only through the use of people skills that the best executives can get employees to deliver excellent results. The best performers are described as follows:

- Even in disagreements, they listen to and respect the ideas of others.
- They are considerate of how their decisions or policies will affect others.
- They are considerate of others' interests when making decisions or formulating policies.

Written comments described the best executives as: "Works with you as opposed to you working for him." "I have never witnessed him ever putting anyone down, even when it's their fault. He will help where needed and even work side-by-side if that is needed."

The worst executives were not viewed positively in terms of people skills: "It is very difficult to discuss problems with him. His favorite line is, 'That's your problem.'" "Even though he compliments employees, it doesn't sound sincere. Was this rehearsed or learned in a management seminar?" "Too many 'cookbook' management techniques." "People don't feel comfortable in his presence."

Leading Change

The ten factors of the most competent executives provide an excellent model for evaluating individual effectiveness. As you read through the descriptions of the best and worst executives, rate yourself on each dimension. You may find some dimensions were not as positive as others. Keep in mind that people typically rate themselves more positively than others do.

If, in your self-evaluation, you feel there are some areas where you need improvement, you may still be a highly effective leader. In our research we found that the best leaders were not perfect in all ten dimensions, but they were very strong in at least seven. Some executives have one extraordinary strength and then back up that strength with very good skills in several other areas. As executives raise their effectiveness in several areas, they also get some halo effect as others begin to rate them higher than they actually are because the executive is so positive in an important dimension. We have also found that people can develop effectiveness in all ten dimensions. The development process requires:

Accurate assessment of current strengths and weaknesses. These skills are only developed when people are clear about where they currently stand. Helping leaders understand their strengths and providing accurate, candid, and regular feedback on where they need to improve is key to increasing effectiveness.

Good coaching and mentoring. Good athletes have good coaches. Good leaders also have good coaches. It's critical in many of these skills that people receive good coaching and mentoring.

Study and training opportunities. Good training programs can help people practice critical skills and understand both the theory and application of each skill of leadership effectiveness. Good leaders are well-studied.

Challenging assignments that provide effective learning environments. Executives may develop these critical skills when they are given assignments in learning environments where it is possible to make mistakes without the loss of position or status. Do-or-die assignments do not provide learning when the unsuccessful individual will be fired.

A "safety net" for people who shouldn't be executives. Many technical professionals take on leadership assignments, only to find they are not as effective as they had hoped to be. Often, they don't even enjoy the work. Organizations can provide meaningful and challenging options for these individuals who can provide technical leadership better than the leadership of people.

APPENDIX

The Readiness for Change Profile

The Readiness for Change Profile assesses individual and organizational readiness for change. The profile looks at several dimensions of individual and organizational readiness. The results may be used to examine your organization's readiness for change and to help people understand what situations make change difficult.

For an accurate assessment, you must answer all the items as honestly and accurately as possible.

Explanation of Terms:

Organization: Refers to the overall organization that is involved in this survey process.

Management: Refers to managers and supervisors in the organization in general.

Work group Identification:

_____

(Name or code number for your work group)

Position (check the box that applies)

❑ Management   ❑ Nonmanagement

Please read the instructions carefully and then complete all the items in the survey.

The following questions provide two statements that are opposite ends of a continuum. Think about your situation in this organization and mark the scale where it best describes you or your current situation. If for some reason you don?t know how to answer an item, please circle the question mark (?) on the right side of the page.

EXAMPLE:

Mark the number which most clearly describes your situation in this organization. Do not circle two numbers or spaces between numbers. If you felt people in the organization generally have adequate work space, you would mark "D".

People are crowded into a small work space.	A	B	C	D	E	People have plenty of space in their work areas.	?

1. It has been hard to recover from mistakes I have made; other people remember them a long time. | A B C D E | I don't seem to be that bothered by making mistakes. I'm able to correct them, recover, and go on. | ?

2. I am frequently overwhelmed by all I am expected to do. | A B C D E | I find it easy to accomplish what I am expected to do. | ?

3. Because of emergencies or problems my work is frequently disorganized. | A B C D E | I carefully plan and organize all of my activities every day and am able to keep to my plan. | ?

4. I am always willing to dig deep and find the extra energy to get big jobs done. | A B C D E | This organization pushes people so hard, so often that I find myself unwilling to take on additional commitments. | ?

5. I usually have a good sense of what's going on in, about, and around the organization. | A B C D E | I feel like I am in the dark most of the time in terms of what is happening in this organization. | ?

6. This organization has a climate where people feel confident to openly express ideas, confront others, and discuss problems among themselves. | A B C D E | This organization has a climate where people tend to keep issues to themselves and not talk about problems. | ?

7. Overall, I feel good about this organization and my place in it. | A B C D E | Overall, I am concerned about the future of this organization and the security of my job. | ?

The following questions provide two statements that are opposite ends of a continuum. Think about your situation in this organization and mark the scale where it best describes you or your current situation.

8. My interactions with people outside my immediate work group are positive and rewarding.

| A | B | C | D | E |

My interactions with people outside my immediate work group too often are negative and draining.

?

9. When I try to do something that is very difficult, I usually think a lot about what will happen if I fail.

| A | B | C | D | E |

When I try to do something that is very difficult, I usually think about how great it will be to succeed.

?

10. Too often I feel frustrated by the end of my day.

| A | B | C | D | E |

I usually feel a positive sense of accomplishment at the end of my day.

?

11. Typically I work in a crisis mode, fighting one fire after another.

| A | B | C | D | E |

I am usually able to plan my work and then work my plan.

?

12. When this organization expects me to give 150%, I usually feel ready and able to do all that I can.

| A | B | C | D | E |

When this organization expects me to give 150%, I usually feel angry; too often this organization takes advantage of me.

?

13. I am kept well informed about changes, new problems or developments that affect me.

| A | B | C | D | E |

Typically, I find out about changes or problems too late for the information to be helpful.

?

14. Top management's actions tend to reinforce a spirit of cooperation between different groups in the organization.

| A | B | C | D | E |

Top management's actions tend to reinforce a spirit of competition between groups and/or people.

?

15. My guess is that this organization will be facing a lot of difficulties and trials in the future.

| A | B | C | D | E |

My guess is that both the organization and I will be successful in the future.

?

16. The people in this organization really care about me and what happens in my life.

| A | B | C | D | E |

The people in this organization are too busy or I'm too busy to get involved.

?

The following questions provide two statements that are opposite ends of a continuum. Think about your situation in this organization and mark the scale where it best describes you or your current situation.

17. It's better to play it safe than to take a risk and fail.	**A** **B** **C** **D** **E**	My motto is "Go for it; nothing ventured, nothing gained." **?**
18. I am expected to do significantly more than I can do and still maintain high quality.	**A** **B** **C** **D** **E**	The amount I am expected to do does not seriously interfere with how well it gets done. **?**
19. I am seldom able to accomplish what I want to in my average working day because of meetings, phone calls, and interruptions.	**A** **B** **C** **D** **E**	I am able to manage my work so that I accomplish what I want to in the average work day. **?**
20. I rarely question the time or effort required in my job.	**A** **B** **C** **D** **E**	The time and effort required of my job seems to be excessive. **?**
21. It is difficult to get management to understand my needs and problems clearly.	**A** **B** **C** **D** **E**	Management takes the time to really listen and understand my point of view. **?**
22. The attitudes of most managers and supervisors might best be described as "trusting people to do a good job without constantly checking up on them."	**A** **B** **C** **D** **E**	The attitudes of most managers and supervisors might best be described as "requiring people to check with managers or supervisors on every aspect of their work." **?**
23. I am confident and optimistic about my future with the organization.	**A** **B** **C** **D** **E**	I am very uncertain about my future with the organization. **?**
24. If there is a tight deadline requiring additional effort from people, the typical approach used in the organization is to push people hard to perform.	**A** **B** **C** **D** **E**	If there is a tight deadline requiring additional effort from people, the typical approach used in the organization is to ask people for their assistance. **?**
25. I like assignments that I know I can do well.	**A** **B** **C** **D** **E**	I like assignments that are highly visible and extremely challenging. **?**

The following questions provide two statements that are opposite ends of a continuum. Think about your situation in this organization and mark the scale where it best describes you or your current situation.

26. I usually find my work extremely challenging and demanding. | A | B | C | D | E | I usually find my work simple and easy. | ? |

27. Too often my work day seems to be one interruption after another. | A | B | C | D | E | I am able to effectively manage my interruptions and distractions. | ? |

28. I frequently feel that I have made a real difference at work. | A | B | C | D | E | I frequently feel like an insignificant cog in a big wheel at work. | ? |

29. People who have different perspectives or opinions are encouraged to express their points of view. | A | B | C | D | E | People who have different perspectives or opinions are discouraged from expressing themselves and their opinions. | ? |

30. I can trust managers and supervisors to be honest with me. | A | B | C | D | E | There is a tendency for managers and supervisors to tell people what they want to hear or be evasive. | ? |

31. I am confident that I can change or resolve most problems and difficulties that I encounter at work. | A | B | C | D | E | I have very little control over most of the problems or difficulties that I encounter at work. | ? |

32. Managers and supervisors tend to be quick to criticize but slow to praise. | A | B | C | D | E | Managers and supervisors tend to be looking for opportunities to recognize individual strengths and accomplishments. | ? |

33. I am willing to try things that are difficult, because even if I fail I usually learn a great deal. | A | B | C | D | E | I avoid doing things where I might fail, because others might think I am stupid. | ? |

34. Sometimes I worry about work to the point that I get frustrated, depressed, or upset. | A | B | C | D | E | Problems or worries at work do not affect my personal life. | ? |

The following questions provide two statements that are opposite ends of a continuum. Think about your situation in this organization and mark the scale where it best describes you or your current situation.

35. I spend too much time doing busy work instead of getting the real job done.

| A | B | C | D | E |

I am able to cut through the red tape to accomplish the most important tasks.

?

36. My attitude toward work might best be described as "work is a very high priority in my life."

| A | B | C | D | E |

My attitude toward work might best be described as "work is important but there are other priorities that require more attention."

?

37. Management appreciates employees who take the initiative to raise issues and focus attention on problems.

| A | B | C | D | E |

The way to get ahead around here is to keep your mouth shut and not rock the boat.

?

38. When the organization shares information, employees typically take the information at face value and assume it is correct.

| A | B | C | D | E |

When the organization shares information, employees are typically skeptical about the information and the intentions of management.

?

39. Frequently problems in this organization turn into unexpected opportunities.

| A | B | C | D | E |

If something can go wrong in this organization, it will.

?

40. When I have a problem on the job, my manager is willing to take time to really listen and thoroughly understand.

| A | B | C | D | E |

When I have a problem on the job, my manager is quick to jump to conclusions and make assumptions that are frequently untrue.

?

Scoring and Interpretation Guide

Section One: Scoring Directions

If you have not had your results computer scored, use the table in Section One to add up your scores on the eight categories.

Section Two: Graphing the Results

Again, if your results have not been computer scored, use Section Two to graph a profile of the eight categories, as well as your individual, organizational, and overall readiness for change. These graphs can also help you to interpret your results.

Section Three: Readiness for Change Model

Section Four: Interpretation of Results

This section gives a detailed description of the meaning of high and low scores.

Section One
SCORING DIRECTIONS

Go through each of your answers and circle an A,B,D, or E answer to each item—answers C and ? don't count. See the example below. Write the corresponding number in the appropriate positive or negative column. For each column, the left column is negative and the right column is positive for each answer. Then simply add up the scores.

An Example

(−)	-2	-1	1	2	(+)
-2	(A)	B	D	E	
	A	B	(D)	E	+1
	A	B	D	(E)	+2
-1	A	(B)	D	E	
-1	D	(E)	A	B	
-4		**Total= -1**			+3

A. Willingness to Risk/Initiate

	(−) -2 -1 1 2 (+)
1.	A B D E
9.	A B D E
17.	A B D E
25.	A B D E
33.	D E A B
	Total=

B. Not Overburdened Overwhelmed

	(−) -2 -1 1 2 (+)
2.	A B D E
10.	A B D E
18.	A B D E
26.	A B D E
34.	A B D E
	Total=

C. Efficiency and Organization

	(−) -2 -1 1 2 (+)
3.	A B D E
11.	A B D E
19.	A B D E
27.	A B D E
35.	A B D E
	Total=

D. Commitment

	(−) -2 -1 1 2 (+)
4.	D E A B
12.	D E A B
20.	D E A B
28.	D E A B
36.	D E A B
	Total=

E. Informed/ Involved

	(−) -2 -1 1 2 (+)
5.	D E A B
13.	D E A B
21.	A B D E
29.	D E A B
37.	D E A B
	Total=

F. High Level of Trust

	(−) -2 -1 1 2 (+)
6.	D E A B
14.	D E A B
22.	D E A B
30.	D E A B
38.	D E A B
	Total=

G. Optimism

	(−) -2 -1 1 2 (+)
7.	D E A B
15.	A B D E
23.	D E A B
31.	D E A B
39.	D E A B
	Total=

H. Supportive Relationships

	(−) -2 -1 1 2 (+)
8.	D E A B
16.	D E A B
24.	A B D E
32.	A B D E
40.	D E A B
	Total=

Section Two
Chart Your Score
(EXAMPLE)

PERCENTILE	5th	10th	25th	50th	75th	90th	95th	
A. Fear of Failure	-10 to -3	-2 to -1	0 to +1	+2 to +3	+4 to +5	+6 to +8	+9 to +10	Willingness to Risk/Initiative
B. Overburdened Overwhelmed	-10 to -6	-5 to -4	-3 to -2	-1 to +1	+2 to +3	+4 to +5	+6 to +10	Not Overburdened/ Overwhelmed
C. Inefficient and Disorganized	-10 to -6	-5 to -4	-3 to -2	-1 to +2	+3 to +4	+5 to +6	+7 to +10	Efficiency and Organization
D. Lack of Commitment	-10 to -3	-2 to -1	0 to +1	+2 to +3	+4 to +5	+6 to +7	+8 to +10	Commitment
E. Uninformed Uninvolved	-10 to -5	-4 to -3	-2 to -1	0 to +2	+3 to +4	+5 to +6	+7 to +10	Informed/ Involved
F. Low Level of Trust	-10 to -4	-3 to -2	-1 to 0	+1 to +3	+4 to +5	+6 to +7	+8 to +10	High Level of Trust
G. Pessimism	-10 to -4	-3 to -2	-1 to 0	+1 to +4	+5 to +6	+7 to +8	+9 to +10	Optimism
H. Unsupportive Relationship	-10 to -3	-2 to -1	0 to +1	+2 to +3	+4 to +5	+6 to +7	+8 to +10	Supportive Relationships

Section Two
Chart Your Score

PERCENTILE	5th	10th	25th	50th	75th	90th	95th	
A. Fear of Failure	-10 to -3	-2 to -1	0 to +1	+2 to +3	+4 to +5	+6 to +8	+9 to +10	Willingness to Risk/Initiative
B. Overburdened Overwhelmed	-10 to -6	-5 to -4	-3 to -2	-1 to +1	+2 to +3	+4 to +5	+6 to +10	Not Overburdened/ Overwhelmed
C. Inefficient and Disorganized	-10 to -6	-5 to -4	-3 to -2	-1 to +2	+3 to +4	+5 to +6	+7 to +10	Efficiency and Organization
D. Lack of Commitment	-10 to -3	-2 to -1	0 to +1	+2 to +3	+4 to +5	+6 to +7	+8 to +10	Commitment
E. Uninformed Uninvolved	-10 to -5	-4 to -3	-2 to -1	0 to +2	+3 to +4	+5 to +6	+7 to +10	Informed/ Involved
F. Low Level of Trust	-10 to -4	-3 to -2	-1 to 0	+1 to +3	+4 to +5	+6 to +7	+8 to +10	High Level of Trust
G. Pessimism	-10 to -4	-3 to -2	-1 to 0	+1 to +4	+5 to +6	+7 to +8	+9 to +10	Optimism
H. Unsupportive Relationship	-10 to -3	-2 to -1	0 to +1	+2 to +3	+4 to +5	+6 to +7	+8 to +10	Supportive Relationships

Section Three: Readiness for Change Model

An individual's readiness for change is influenced by two primary factors. The first is individual readiness. This includes a set of personal characteristics, attitudes, and values that tend to facilitate change. These are:

- Willingness to take risks and initiative
- Not overburdened or overwhelmed
- Efficiency and organization
- Commitment

The second factor is organizational readiness. This involves a set of organizational characteristics that reinforce change:

- Informed and involved
- High level of trust
- Optimism
- Supportive relationships

Forces in organizations tend to bring the two factors into equilibrium. For example, if the organization supports change by trusting employees to take risks, individuals tend to reciprocate by actually taking the initiative to make changes. On the other hand, organizations with a low level of trust tend to discourage people from taking risks. From the individual readiness perspective, people who feel optimistic tend to feel less overwhelmed by what is required of them. Their personal commitment is enhanced by supportive relationships they experience in organizations. Likewise, people who can manage efficiently tend to build organizational optimism.

Because the two factors of the equation tend to move to equilibrium, it is possible to increase the overall readiness for change by increasing one of the factors. If organizations work to keep their employees better informed and to demonstrate an increased level of trust, the individuals in those organizations will respond by showing increased commitment and more of a willingness to take risks.

Section Four: Interpretation of Scores

This survey measures eight characteristics that are related to a person's readiness for change. Some items deal with individual readiness, while others deal with the organizational readiness for change. Together the scores provide an overall readiness for change profile.

Although the scores are displayed as positive and negative, low scores should not be viewed as bad or that a person has failed in some way. Scores simply show preferences.

Willingness to Risk and Initiate

Low scores. A low score indicates that a person does not want to make mistakes. Past mistakes haunt the person, and he or she often thinks about the dangers of "blowing it." This person understands his or her limitations very well, and is not willing to push beyond these limits.

High scores. A high score shows people feel they can try difficult things with success, while accepting and learning from honest mistakes. These people will push their limits and focus on the potential rewards rather than the possibility of failure.

Not Overburdened or Overwhelmed

Low scores. These people have a difficult time handling the demands placed upon them; they are often expected to do more than they want to do. Interruptions or distractions disproportionately disrupt their normal workflow. They constantly feel frustrated by their work.

High scores. People feel they can accomplish what is required and that they can negotiate priorities if necessary. They take interruptions in stride and are able and willing to make significant contributions in spite of many demands.

Efficiency and Organization

Low scores. A low score indicates people are working in a crisis mode. They often waste time on things that are unimportant, they are late to appointments, and they are unable to accomplish much of real significance.

High scores. These people are able to plan and organize their day while managing interruptions and distractions. They allow necessary time to do the job right, and are punctual in their appointments and assignments.

Commitment to Work

Low scores. Indicate that people feel rather insignificant at work. They have a low sense of control, are very flexible and adaptive, and they let things happen rather than make things happen. Other parts of their lives are equal in importance to work.

High scores. Here they generally indicate that people feel energized by their work; they believe in their own abilities and they are dependable. They can push themselves hard and do whatever is necessary to get things done. Their work is very important to them.

Informed and Involved

Low scores. People feel they don't have a handle on what is going on in the organization. They have difficulty in communicating and getting clear answers. There is a consequent lack of trust in others.

High scores. These people are well informed and have access to the information they need. They believe information is communicated honestly and have experienced commitment and involvement from all levels of the organization.

Level of Trust

Low scores. Low scores generally show that people tend to keep problems to themselves. These people experience negative competition and constant supervision. They believe people tell them only what they want to hear.

High scores. High scores show that people feel free to openly discuss issues and to solve problems publicly. They experience a sense of cooperation and freedom. They are not over-supervised and they feel the company has their best interest at heart.

Optimism

Low scores. Low scores here indicate that people are uncertain about the future and are concerned about their security. They feel they have little control over problems and they often expect things to go wrong.

High scores. People with high scores feel good about their past contributions, their present status, and their future potential and the company. They are confident about their ability to solve problems and to make a difference.

Supportive Relationships

Low scores. Here they indicate that people have negative interactions with people; they are distant or don't treat one another well. They experience criticism and don't feel others listen to them.

High scores. These people experience positive and rewarding interactions with others. People care about them, they are willing to help, and their strengths and accomplishments are recognized.

ABOUT THE AUTHOR

 *Joe Folkman is a founding principal* of Novations Group, Inc., where he helps organizations design assessment tools and feedback processes for organizational and individual improvement. He has over twenty years of experience in survey research, analysis, and consulting in organizational diagnosis, management assessment, customer service analysis, and managing both large-scale and individual change processes. He has developed measurement tools to assess an organization's strategic alignment and its readiness for change.

Folkman is the author of *Turning Feedback into Change,* and *Making Feedback Work,* and he has received a masters degree in organizational behavior and a doctorate in social and organizational psychology from Brigham Young University. He has conducted extensive research in psychometrics, survey research, statistical analysis of survey data, and organizational and individual change. His research has been published in the *Wall Street Journal, Personnel,* and *Executive Excellence,* among other publications, and he has designed and written numerous software programs to help companies gather and analyze feedback survey data.

For over twenty years, Joe has consulted with a variety of top companies around the world, including Amoco, Boeing, Canadian Imperial Bank of Commerce, Cisco Systems, Eaton, Exxon, General Mills, Hewlett-Packard, McGraw-Hill, Mobil, Nortel, Novell, Phillips Petroleum, Rockwell, and Weyerhaueser.

He lives in Orem, Utah, with his wife, Laura, and their five children: Brandon, Rachel, BreAnne, Matthew, and Corbin.

Novations Group, Inc.
(A PROVANT Company)

Novations Group, Inc., is a founding member of PROVANT, Inc., an international consulting and training organization consisting of fourteen affiliated firms with expertise in such areas as communication, diversity, multimedia learning, retail sales training, human resource management, and behavioral sciences. Novations is a rapidly growing strategy and human resource management consulting firm with offices in New York, Texas, and Utah. Its mission is to develop individual capability while achieving business results. For over 20 years it has been serving some of the best companies in North America and Europe in areas of strategy clarification, organizational design, and competency. As one of the largest corporate survey firms in the nation, Novations is perhaps best known for its 360-degree surveys and organizational assessments. The company has emerged as an industry leader in providing a broad range of helpful survey and profile instruments for individuals and companies including:

Organization Assessments
Organizational Analysis Survey
Strategic Alignment Survey
Total Quality Survey
Customer Service Survey

Management and Leadership Development
Managing Individual and Team Effectiveness
360-Degree Competency Profiles
Customized Leadership Profiles

Team Assessments
Team Development Survey
Team Effectiveness Profile

Novations' surveys and profiles consist of both written and numerical response data. In addition to unlimited demographic comparisons, the company's extensive database allows for surveys to be compared with national, company, group, and industry norms where available. Support services include customization of standardized instruments, survey administration, Internet and on-line data processing, data interpretation, presentation of results and recommendations, and development of activities such as strategic alignment and long-term planning.

To obtain customized feedback surveys for organizational assessment, individual profiles and analysis, or to receive information on Novations' workshops and conferences, please contact:

Novations Group, Inc.
5314 North 250 West, Suite 320
Provo, UT 84604
phone: (801) 375-7525
fax: (801) 375-7595
www.novations.com

Since 1984, *Executive Excellence* has provided business leaders and managers with the best and latest thinking on leadership development, managerial effectiveness, and organizational productivity. Each issue is filled with insights and answers from top business executives, trainers, and consultants—information you won't find in any other publication.

"Excellent! This is one of the finest newsletters I've seen in the field."

—Tom Peters, co-author of *In Search of Excellence*

"Executive Excellence *is the* Harvard Business Review *in* USA Today *format.*"

—Stephen R. Covey, author of *The 7 Habits of Highly Effective People*

"Executive Excellence *is the best executive advisory newsletter anywhere in the world—it's just a matter of time before a lot more people find that out.*"

—Ken Blanchard, co-author of *The One-Minute Manager*

CONTRIBUTING EDITORS INCLUDE

Stephen R. Covey

Ken Blanchard

Marjorie Blanchard

Charles Garfield

Peter Senge

Gifford Pinchot

Elizabeth Pinchot

Warren Bennis

Brian Tracy

Kevin Cashman

Denis Waitley

For more information about *Executive Excellence* or *Personal Excellence*, or for information regarding books, audio tapes, CD-ROMs, custom editions, reprints, and other products, please call Executive Excellence Publishing at:

1-800-304-9782

or visit our web site: **http://www.eep.com**

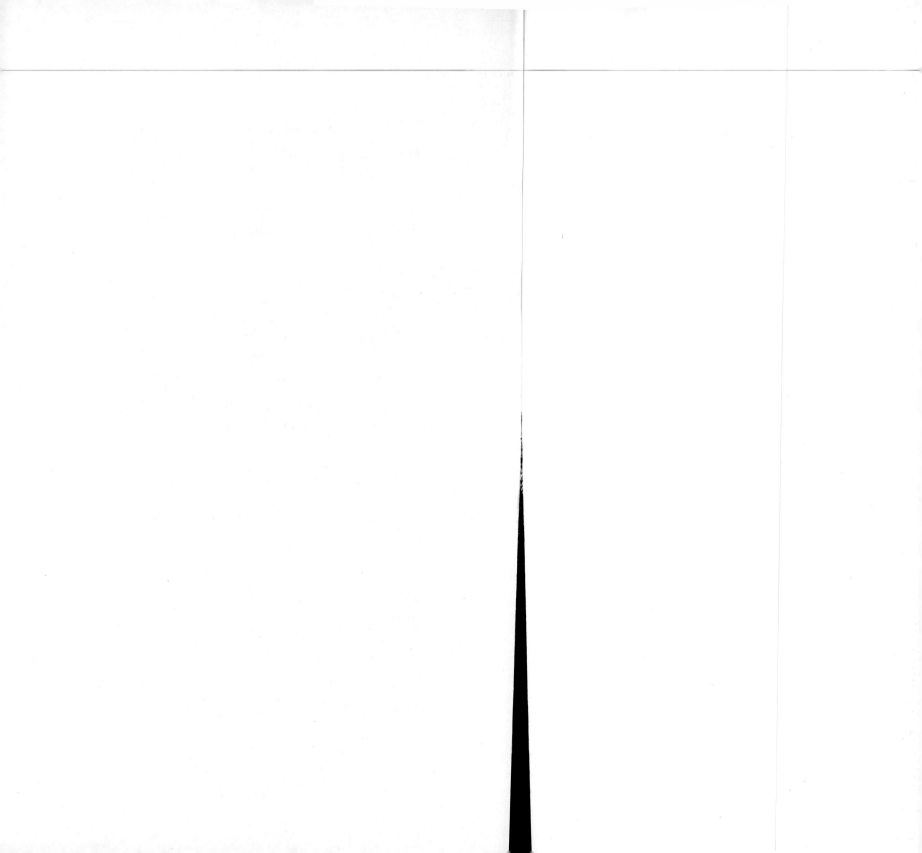

Executive Excellence

Since 1984, *Executive Excellence* has provided business leaders and managers with the best and latest thinking on leadership development, managerial effectiveness, and organizational productivity. Each issue is filled with insights and answers from top business executives, trainers, and consultants—information you won't find in any other publication.

"Excellent! This is one of the finest newsletters I've seen in the field."

—Tom Peters, co-author of *In Search of Excellence*

"Executive Excellence *is the* Harvard Business Review *in* USA Today *format."*

—Stephen R. Covey, author of *The 7 Habits of Highly Effective People*

"Executive Excellence *is the best executive advisory newsletter anywhere in the world—it's just a matter of time before a lot more people find that out."*

—Ken Blanchard, co-author of *The One-Minute Manager*

CONTRIBUTING EDITORS INCLUDE

Stephen R. Covey

Ken Blanchard

Marjorie Blanchard

Charles Garfield

Peter Senge

Gifford Pinchot

Elizabeth Pinchot

Warren Bennis

Brian Tracy

Kevin Cashman

Denis Waitley

For more information about *Executive Excellence* or *Personal Excellence*, or for information regarding books, audio tapes, CD-ROMs, custom editions, reprints, and other products, please call Executive Excellence Publishing at:

1-800-304-9782
or visit our web site: http://www.eep.com